The Reanimation of Malcom

The Reanimation of Malcom

The Little Book of Modern Times

Patrick Lawrence O'Malley

Tampa, Florida

The views and opinions expressed in this book are solely those of the author and do not reflect the views or opinions of Gatekeeper Press. Gatekeeper Press is not to be held responsible for and expressly disclaims responsibility for the content herein.

The Reanimation of Malcom:
The Little Book of Modern Times

Published by Gatekeeper Press
7853 Gunn Hwy., Suite 209
Tampa, FL 33626
www.GatekeeperPress.com

Copyright © 2023 by Patrick Lawrence O'Malley

All rights reserved. Neither this book, nor any parts within it may be sold or reproduced in any form or by any electronic or mechanical means, including information storage and retrieval systems, without permission in writing from the author. The only exception is by a reviewer, who may quote short excerpts in a review.

The editorial work for this book is entirely the product of the author. Gatekeeper Press did not participate in and is not responsible for any aspect of this element.

Library of Congress Control Number: (adding in later)

ISBN (paperback): 9781662946257
ISBN (hardcover): 9781662952074
eISBN: 9781662946264

GARDEN RUBBISH
Featuring the Reanimation of Malcom

A seventy-year-old man is looking on his iPad for the telephone number of his local council garden waste department. He locates the number, saying, "Ahh." He dials the number and talks to a waste department rep, saying, "I'd called a couple of days ago to see if my garden rubbish would be picked up, as I had just paid for the service the previous week."

The lady on the other side of the phone said that it would be in the system by now, so there shouldn't be a problem.

The old man replied, "Well, that's not the case, as this is what happened: the collection vehicle just drove by and left it on the end of my driveway."

The rep said she would see if it's in the system and then, returning, said, "It's not on the system yet, although it should've been within two days of paying for the service."

So I said to her that they better come back and pick it up. She replied that they wouldn't be able to do anything about that until two more weeks had passed and they would be due again to retrieve garden waste. So I said to her that if they didn't come back and pick it up today that I would dump it on the street; she said, "If you do that, you will be breaking a bylaw and be in violation," so I said okay and hung up. And I thought for a few seconds and said to myself, "Oh, I'll call back and see what she's got to say about this."

So I phoned back and said, "Now instead of dumping the garden rubbish on the street, since I have a steep driveway, I'll just dump it at the bottom of the driveway a few feet away from the street and then ask the Lord to send a storm big enough to wash it into the street, and I'll film the event on my phone, so you can't cite me for the garden rubbish."

The lady replied, "Oh, so you're simply going to ask God to send a storm just like that and expect it to happen?"

The old man replied, "Yes, of course, absolutely certain, no doubt about it whatsoever!"

So she says, "How are you so certain about this, Mr. O'Malley?"

"Well, I will tell you a bit of my story if you have the time."

She said, "It's very quiet today, so yeah, tell me your story. I want to know why you're so certain about being able to do such a thing."

So, I told her my story about the Reanimation of Malcom and the little book called Modern Times contained within the story.

Introducing:
The Reanimation of Malcom

Hello, reader; this story is entitled: "The Reanimation of Malcom." First and foremost, this story is entirely true, consisting of phenomena, spiritual phenomenon, and modern-day prophecy from the mid 1980s to the near-past with all of the events mentioned already having been fulfilled, acts of faith having not been seen or performed for hundreds or thousands of years, some perhaps never to have been recorded. The author is a totally unaffiliated, born-again-by-the-will-and-grace-of-God Christian, untied to any church other than God's spiritual church that exists outside of the physical dimension. Every named person is genuine and a witness of these events described and prophesied. These acts of faith take place primarily in England, California, Indiana, Arizona, and various other locations. There is some legal documentation, approximately one hundred pages, submitted to a magistrate's court in Gateshead, England, and a further separate one hundred pages submitted to an industrial tribunal court in Leeds, England, to support the facts of this story. For example: the act of a prophesied lightning strike, stating the time, place, effect, and outcome, with transcriptions being submitted for a court appearance on December 19th, 2004, to Gateshead magistrates court, seen by Judge Raymond Watson, referring to the lightning prophecy and other events whereby they accused myself of having special powers because of the common knowledge of the lightning prediction in the factory and other acts of faith that they were made aware of and therefore felt threatened and intimidated by my presence at our place of mutual employment, their words; not mine. Where my response was, I do not have any special powers, although I do have faith, strength, and power in righteousness through God's grace. This story is for the purpose of restoring and building faith in God and in Jesus's name and to validate the scripture in the book of Revelation, stating: "For the testimony of Jesus is the spirit of prophecy."

This story opens with a mood-setting collection of lyrics written in the summer of 1992 in Bodmin, Cornwall, England, as follows:

A season of summer invades winter's domain
A flood threatens from its dark icy terrain
An exodus of nomads crowd into the playgrounds
The foraging for delight spawns an eerie fright
Echo from the mountain bound across man's insight
The darkness chimed who's next in line
Morals decline but the money's all mine
The poster cries wanted dead not alive
It looks like the haunted time has arrived
The mourning for ashes will follow soon
The clashing of symbols bellow out doom
The cloak of confusion paves a dark way
Preceding the message placed in the grave
As the grim reaper appoints the final day
Man's hourglass gets trapped in the corridor of lies

Confused minds play host as the nightmare thrives
There's a reception being held in the foyer of tied limbs
To celebrate the race staged on a track of quicksand
As the picture clears a dark evil creature appears
Stands poised with a branding iron in his hand
Ready to inflict the desired number of man
And the darkness chimes, who's next in line?

Thank you very much for your interest.

Yours sincerely,

Patrick Lawrence O'Malley

PART ONE

The Beginning

Late October/Early November 1991: Meeting Adolfo

Patrick is arriving outside of the Cafe Roma on Rodeo Drive in Bel Air and walks in with a friend, an artist and master engraver, Armandina Lozano, considered one of the top three engravers in the world, with whom Patrick had been working, writing lyrics for her personal book of engravings, a long-term project that she has been working on. She introduces Patrick and Adolfo Bringas to each other. Adolfo is playing a grand piano and singing to the patrons. He eventually invites Patrick to sing with him at the piano, which he does. So, Adolfo then plays a blues riff and asks Patrick to ad-lib some lyrics, and he will sing along for a few verses. Patrick agrees and thinks up a few verses on the spot, and the two of them perform together for a minute or two. Then the two of them sit down with Armandina during Adolfo's break and discuss lyrical ideas for a collaboration with Adolfo and the band that he is putting together. So, Patrick compiles a list of key words for conceptional songs while at Cafe Roma to take home with him.

Patrick then meets up with Adolfo at Nicky Blair's on Sunset Boulevard a few nights later at this private club, where a person would have to knock on the door and be questioned by security if they didn't recognize you. You would have to tell security who you were and who you were there to see. Once you had been vouched for, you would be shown into the club. And after that, you would be let in straightaway. Adolfo introduces Patrick to Danny Huston and Tony Curtis by their first names only. They are seated at the table just in front of the piano that Adolfo is playing and singing with to the patrons. Patrick sits at the table with Danny and Tony, conversing with them that night and two times a week for the next six weeks at Nicky Blair's and twice a week at Cafe Roma. Meeting at night after work and at the weekend parties that were held almost exclusively at Armandina's condo in Beverly Hills, Patrick developed a friendship with Raul, a very talented musician, and became very friendly with Tony, the three of them talking about life in London, England, in the seventies. And meeting with the rest of the prospective members of the new band while constructing the songs for the demo, in which Brad Fiedel had put the finishing guitars and all the production and engineering work on the demo in his studio, in his house in Hollywood.

The Inspiration: A Couple of Weeks after Meeting Adolfo

Patrick is at the home of Daniel Huston, also known as Danny, an actor and director in his own right. Patrick has accompanied a Mr. Adolfo Bringas and another lad called Daniel Cammie. Adolfo is a very good friend of Danny. Daniel knows Danny very well through his association with Danny's father and asks Danny if he would put the video on for Patrick. The video is a family piece depicting Danny's father, Mr. John Huston. The film is an exposè in the form of an interview with the director on set, with clips being shown during the narration, featuring some of the films that he had been involved with, including *The Bible,* which he directed, although he mainly spoke about other Bible stories and similar films such as *Ben Hur* and *Spartacus*. At the end of the short film, John Huston is saying how much he enjoyed being involved with these movies and the movies from the Bible stories, but what he would really like to see is a modern and current biblical movie depicting what God is up to now, perhaps with His own modern-day prophet.

Meeting Malcom: The Night after Meeting Adolfo

Patrick is on the balcony of his cousin Michell's condominium on Sepulveda Boulevard in North Hills, California. Since the day after he met Adolfo at the Cafe Roma, he's been writing lyrics on a dozen different concepts for an album collaboration with Adolfo and his new band. Patrick is an American who's been living in England for the past nineteen years. Patrick started writing lyrics mid-morning and now has run out of the cigarettes that he had been using to make English-style joints with, to smoke while writing his lyrics, so he decides to walk to a local 7-Eleven store to get some more cigarettes. It was about three in the morning when Patrick left his cousin's house, there was nobody on the street, and not even a car driving past, the only other people around were the employees working in the 7-Eleven store, the pizza shop, the donut shop, and also at the gas station across the street.

He walks to the store, gets the cigarettes, and walks back towards the condo, where he sees a man approaching him on the sidewalk from the opposite direction, about half of the distance back to the condo. The man stops to ask Patrick where he is.

He says in a polite manner, "Excuse me, sir, I've just arrived here, and I don't really know where I am; could you please tell me the name of this place?"

Patrick is thinking, I know that situation myself, and replies, "Of course, this is North Hills in the San Fernando Valley in Los Angeles County.

The man says, "Which way is Los Angeles?"

Patrick points southward towards LA and says, "About twenty miles that way."

The man then asked Patrick if he could have a cigarette; Patrick had the packet in his left hand and replied, "Of course," and offered him a cigarette and gave him a light, and then a conversation ensued. The man started telling his story to Patrick of how he had been the son of a Baptist lay preacher and was a Christian for some time and had then converted to the Islamic faith and, in time, he had come to the conclusion that no matter what, eventually a man would have to use violence and kill or be killed; there was no escape from this. Patrick argued that that conclusion was not the truth, and a man could refrain from using violence according to his faith in God. Patrick and the man talked and walked around the shops and smoked a few cigarettes while doing so, momentarily stopping, and stood talking further about this subject.

Patrick said, "I know that there is a religion of hatred practiced by some, but not all Islamic sects, but those that do, should consider this: It is said that 'Mohammed ascended into heaven from Temple Mount, the place that is now called the Dome of the Rock, to go before the Almighty and receive his blessing.' Does anyone truly believe that Mohammed ascended into heaven wearing a cloak of hatred and violence enclosed in his mantle and in his heart as he approached the presence of the Almighty, who is also the God of love. Those who embrace hatred and violence worship the spirit of evil, which is satanic! And therefore are not true to the faith of Mohammad or to the God of Israel, and that also applies to those that follow the faith of Jesus, and those that do embrace these ethics have been deceived by their ill-informed teachers, who are very obviously satanic and agents of the devil, out to deceive and to try to capture the righteous souls of the innocent. Furthermore, the term *jihad*, or holy war, is a contradiction because all and any other description of war is not justified. The only real jihad is the war that is taking place in the realm and dimension of the spirit and within the kingdom of heaven. As the scripture says: ‘And there was war in heaven, Michael and his angels fought, and the Devil and his angels fought, and Michael and his angels prevailed against them and the Devil and his angels were cast down unto the Earth.’ Which will happen very soon. Therefore, every act of war on earth is unholy and an act of evil hatred inspired by Satanic forces. This applies to every religion that promotes war and violence. And every individual that partakes in these acts of violence, it says, be not deceived and be assured, God is not mocked, as the commandment says: Thou shall not kill, period, no exception! Wisdom states that it is impossible for someone who has been filled with the Holy Spirit of God to harbor hatred, violence, racism, and the other fruits of evil in their hearts. For if they truly are in possession of God’s Holy Spirit, then there is no room left in their hearts and minds for such evil to influence their being. Know this now that the time of judgment is nigh and fast-approaching, even at the doors, ready to knock the doors of false perception into hell!”

Nonetheless, after approximately an hour of conversation about this issue, Patrick and the man could not come to a mutual agreement on the subject that they had been discussing as they walked around the area where the shops were located. They then stopped and stood near the corner of the intersection on Sepulveda Boulevard and had come to a total impasse.

Just then, some of the lyrics that Patrick had written earlier came to mind. So, Patrick said to him, "I want you to look into my eyes and meditate on these words that I am about to tell you: 'If you listen to my eyes, you will hear what I have seen, and you will see what I have heard, the key is in the Word.'"

The man said "okay" and stood still and looked into his eyes as Patrick meditated on what he wanted him to see and understand. So, he asked the Lord to show him, in a moment in time, the history and the future of his faith and who his friends and allies are in the kingdom of God, and these are the things that he saw:

Malcom's Vision: Listen to My Eyes—an Enlightenment to Absorb July 1970: The Beginning of a Moment in Time

In the vision that followed, Malcom saw Patrick as an eighteen-year-old talking to two sisters, Claudia and Laura, aged about seventeen and eighteen, in an apartment located on Saticoy Street in Van Nuys, California, at approximately 10:30 a.m. Patrick was telling them what he had been up to in Northern California, as he had just arrived back to the San Fernando Valley the previous evening after traveling for about six or seven weeks and spending the last couple of weeks on the beach, on the northern side of the mouth of the Russian River in Northern California.

The girls asked him what he was doing there; Patrick replied, "Well, when I first got down onto the beach, I saw a dozen or more huts made of driftwood, so my friend Sam and I gathered some driftwood as well and built a hut to camp in, and then we partied with the other hippies that were chilling there, and I did also spend a lot of time meditating on what my life would be like in the latter days leading to the second coming of Jesus Christ."

They both said together, "Oh, you believe in Jesus then?"

Patrick replied, "I always have, but recently I have felt His presence much closer than ever before."

"Well, then what do you think about UFOs?"

Patrick replied, "I think that they are a manifestation of something from a different dimension that we can see momentarily every now and then." Patrick paused to have a drink from his cup of coffee and said, "And oh, by the way, we are going to see one tonight. When we leave here to go and meet my brother, we will stop walking suddenly, when we get to the vacant lot next to the Saticoy Pines. Then we will, the three of us, stop, and we won't even say a word at all to each other. We will just turn towards the empty field and look up into the sky in unison. There we will see what will look like a cloud formation that will look like a cross. After a moment, it will descend towards us and get brighter and sharper in its formation as it gets closer and then shall linger there for a short time and then disappear. As evening descended, I observed this phenomenon unfold and play out, as foretold by Patrick.

Early November 1973: Leaving London and Finding the Umbrella of Grace

Patrick is now in England, three years later, as a passenger in a car with his newlywed English wife, June, having hitchhiked from London. They're now being dropped off underneath the slipway exit for Luton in an absolutely thunderous rainstorm, with the sky being filled with very dark clouds. The amount of rain is so heavy that it's almost like the intensity of being underneath a waterfall.

June, Patrick's bride of a few months, asked him, "So what are we going to do now?"

Patrick said, "You wait here, I'm going to ask Jesus to make a hole in the clouds and to create an umbrella of grace so I can remain dry until a ride picks us up. You stay here until the car stops, and I'll wave for you to come to the slip road. You're going to have to run from under this shelter to the dry spot, okay?

June replied, "Alright, I'll wait here."

Patrick walked towards the edge of the underpass, stopped, bowed his head, and prayed to the Lord, saying, "Jesus, will you please create an umbrella of grace and make a hole in the clouds to create a dry environment for me to stand in while I wait for a car to stop and pick us up? Thank you Lord."

Patrick then ran through the teeming rain to the slip road entrance of the motorway and stopped and immediately looking upward, he saw the sunshine radiating through a small hole in the clouds right over the place where he stood, absolutely dry and bathed in sunlight within a radius of about forty feet, raising his arms towards heaven, saying: "Wow, yeah, what amazing grace, hallelujah Lord, thank you Jesus!"

When a car stopped after fifteen minutes or so, Patrick spoke to the driver and his passenger, saying, "My wife is at the underpass sheltering; I'll wave her over if that's okay."

The driver replied, "Of course."

Patrick waved to June to beckon her over to the car. Patrick and June got into the backseat of the Morris Minor. The car drove onward on the slip road and onto the northbound side of the motorway.

After another quarter of an hour or so, the driver spoke, saying that something was driving him absolutely nuts, to the point where he said, "I couldn't stop wondering how this could even happen."

Patrick asked him and said, "What do you mean by 'how this could even have happened,' and what exactly is bothering you?"

He said he couldn't get the sound of the windscreen wipers scraping against the dry windscreen out of his head. "Just where you had been hitchhiking." And he said, "How long were you waiting there, and furthermore, that heavy rain had been pouring down unrelentingly all the way from London until we stopped just there, at the slip road, where it seemed to be like a small shelter had been erected over you and kept you completely dry until you and your missus got into the car, and we drove off. Then the rain started again immediately as we drove off; it was not dry anywhere except where you were standing, and you're even drier than your missus."

Patrick said, "Oh, dude, sorry, that's my fault, I was waiting for roughly fifteen to twenty minutes, and you're right, it was pouring down really heavily all the way from Shepherd's Bush to Luton, where our last lift dropped us off under that bridge." Then he said, "I'm a Christian."

The driver said, "I don't believe in church."

Patrick replied, "I'm not that kind of Christian; I don't go to any particular church; the Bible says that God does not dwell in a temple made with hands, for the body has been prepared to become a temple to worship God; therefore, I am in church at every breathing moment as Jesus said that the kingdom of God is not either here nor there but within this body that has been created. Therefore, I believe in living by faith every day. This has been my outlook ever since the moment that I came to realize that I need a miracle or something like a miracle every day, just to get through each day with all the questions that we face in life; as we all know, life can be very hard at times, dude. So, I asked God to create the solution to the stormy dilemma facing a hitchhiker in a potentially very wet situation.

"As you can see that I don't have an umbrella, therefore I asked Jesus to create an umbrella of grace and to make a hole in the clouds to keep me dry while we waited for you to pick us up. And that's what happened. And I honestly fully expected it to happen because I really needed a lend of an umbrella, and I only had God to turn to, to solve this dilemma. And I know that I must always expect to receive my supplication fulfilled, otherwise there wouldn't be any point in asking, without faith. And because I'm a human that has had an encounter with Jesus that caused me to become a born-again Christian and henceforth living by faith. And that is why I must have a very simple attitude about what faith is. Believe before you ask that you have already achieved the solution and the answer, for whatever reason that you felt a need that would cause you to reach out to the Almighty. And that is why God answered my prayer. And I absolutely loved His response; it was so cool to see that sunny dry spot that I prayed for! What a hallelujah that is, my friends!" And you know what else dude, all the true followers of Jesus can embrace that same umbrella of grace. And those also that have a deep desire to find grace will find grace. It's a gift that God is willing to give readily.

Back in Time
March 1971: Undercover Hippies in the Valley and on the Road

Patrick is at work at his Uncle Cappy's automotive center. Cappy hired a new mechanic, a French-Canadian young man called Pierre. Cappy said to Patrick, "You two can live together in that two-bedroom bungalow situated towards the back of the property," behind the garage where they worked. Cappy also said, "Since Pierre can't speak English, you're going to have to teach him the language; you can both live there rent-free as part of your wages."

Now, Pierre had long hair and a beard and so did Patrick. After a couple of months, Cappy started to bitch about the long hair, and after a few days of bitching, Cappy stated that he would give both a pay raise if they did something about the hair. Patrick and Pierre talked it over that night after work. Both agreed that cutting their hair is a definite no-go, so one of them came up with the idea to go to Hollywood and purchase a couple of really good wigs to conceal the long hair. They went to Hollywood that Saturday and spent a week's wage each on some very realistic toupees. After a couple of weeks, Pierre's brother and his cousin Andre arrived from Quebec to stay in California for a vacation break. In the meantime, Patrick and Pierre were getting away with the wigs that were extremely realistic, and Cappy did not have any idea that they hadn't had their hair cut at all. After a couple of weeks, the boys reminded Cappy about the pay raise deal that he had made with them. Cappy was not prepared to keep to his word. After another week, the two of them approached Cappy yet again about the pay raise, which Cappy refused to honor, so the two declared in harmony that they quit and removed their wigs and left their jobs.

In the meantime, before they quit, Patrick was opening a letter; it was from the draft board informing him of his conscription and his draft card, containing his nineteenth birthday lottery number for the 1971 draft. Patrick read the draft card, saying out loud to himself, "Fuck this, I'm not killing anyone at all for any reason," and then unceremoniously put the draft card into the trash can. He then told his friend Pierre about the letter from the draft board and said that he would definitely go with him to Connecticut. Later, Patrick found out that his draft card number had become exempt, some years later, because of a congressional inquiry into the legality of the lottery system to determine the constitutional validity of the system, which resulted in six numbers being exempted, as the lottery was already in operation. Thereby he avoided the prospect of going to Vietnam, although unaware of this fact for some eight to ten years.

And in the meantime, while the guys were waiting for their pay raise, when Pierre's brother and cousin had arrived from Montreal for their vacation in California, they had stayed with the guys for a couple of weeks while the long-hair dilemma was going on, until a few days after the wig drop with Pat's uncle. Then a bit later they got together with Andre and Jean Michael, Pierre's brother, and the four of them took off in an old 51 Chevy, their destination being Waterbury, Connecticut, where Pierre had more family members, where they could stay and find work. The lads got their stuff together for the journey, filled the car up with juice, and the four of them started driving east on Route 66. The four took turns driving and only stopped to fill the gas tank. By the time that they reached Albuquerque, the car's engine threw a rod right through the oil sump pan, and the car came to an immediate stop. The boys got out and pushed the car to the side of the road and got their stuff and broke up into two groups and started to hitchhike. Andre and Jean Michael started to hitchhike first and got a ride within ten minutes. Patrick and Pierre started hitchhiking after they left and got a lift within ten minutes or so. They got dropped off about thirty miles up the road, and Andre and Jean Michael were waiting at the same place hitchhiking. When they saw Patrick and Pierre being dropped off at the same spot, the four of them had a couple of joints and a laugh before resuming the hitchhiking. Andre and Jean Michael went first and got a ride after a few minutes. Patrick and Pierre started hitchhiking and got a ride after ten minutes or so. They got dropped off about another thirty-five miles up the road in the mountain pass on Route 66. As it turned out they got dropped off at the same junction as Andre and Jean Michael, and it was already dark, so the four decided to camp out just off the roadside for the night. Andre had a surprise for Patrick and Pierre; the hippies that gave them their last ride also gave them a tennis-ball-sized lump of red Lebanese hashish, so they had a good smoke that night, adding the red Leb to the weed from Patrick's stash in his sleeping bag.

In the morning, they set out to hitchhike, with Andre and Jean Michael starting first, getting a ride after about ten or fifteen minutes. Now Patrick and Pierre had no luck in getting a lift and waited a good three hours with absolutely no luck. They decided to put their wigs on and try again. This time they got a lift straightaway from a man in his mid-twenties in a red Mustang. He offered the dudes a ride and said, "Hang on a minute while I put this suit in the trunk of the car." The lads said thanks; Pierre got into the passenger seat, and Patrick followed the driver to the trunk and noticed that the suit was a policeman's uniform, and there was a communication setup in the trunk as well. The guys got into the car, and the driver drove back onto the highway and turned the car around at the next junction and drove back to Albuquerque, nearly seventy miles away; he said that he needed to get something from town. At this moment Patrick became a bit wary and a bit paranoid, thinking, oh what's happening here? They arrived in Albuquerque, and the driver pulled into a car park and went into the shop and came back with a fifth bottle of vodka in a paper bag. He got into the driver's seat and reversed into another car that was parked behind us, and then he just shouted a few obscenities and drove off hit-and-run-style, although the other car was empty, so nobody was hurt. We got back onto the highway, and he explained that he was going to his girlfriend's house on the Reservation, and it's about a hundred-and-forty miles east. A conversation ensued where at one point the use of marijuana was discussed, and he had explained how his girlfriend smoked it quite often, and she often tried to get him to try it.

So, Patrick said, "So what do you do when you come across some when you're at work?

He replied, "My girlfriend would dump me if I arrested someone for marijuana, so I take it away from them and let them go and then I just throw it away."

Patrick said, "Well, that's pretty cool, so why did you not try it out for yourself with your girlfriend?"

He said that he did not want to look bad in any way if he couldn't maintain during the effect and then said, "I would have tried it with you guys, as I feel comfortable in your company, but you two obviously are not the hippie types that smoke marijuana, as you both have short hair."

So, Pierre and Patrick looked at each other and nodded to each other and removed their wigs and said, "But we are hippies now, and we have got a little bit of doob with us as well. Do you want to try it, buddy, I have got my pipe in my pocket, shall I fill it up?"

He replied, "Yeah man, I'm ready for it."

After three pipefuls had been passed around, extreme dry mouth set in, so the guys stopped at an Indian curio shop. Patrick and the driver went into the shop, and the driver got three bottles of Coca-Cola and then pulled the three of them together off of the counter and dropped them onto the floor with all three bottles breaking apart, spilling glass and the cola all over the floor. The Navajo gentleman started shouting at us, and David shouted back at him in the Navajo language.

Patrick said, "What did he say?"

David replied, "He said that he was going to call the police, and we better leave, like, right now." David said that he was enjoying our company and said that "The last turn-off we just passed was the road to my girlfriend's house, but I'm going to take you up the highway for another hundred miles," which he did. So, he had to stop for gas along the way. So, he stopped and filled his car with gas and said, "I'm going to get some coke for us."

Pat said, "I'll come in with you, and I'll carry the bottles back to the car."

David said, "I'm alright now; I won't drop them again."

Pat said, "Okay, but I'm going to come in with you, buddy."

So, the two of them went in to pay for the gas and to get the three bottles of cola from the coke machine inside. David grabbed the three bottles and carried them to the counter and paid for them and then carried them out to the car and dropped all three bottles onto the pavement just outside of the car door, and they smashed as they hit the concrete. The garage employee came to the doorway and started shouting in Navajo, then David shouted back to him in Navajo, so Patrick said, "What did he say?"

David said that "He said that he was going to call the cops, so we better get the hell out of here."

They got back into the car, and Pierre said, "Why didn't you carry the cokes, Patrick?"

He said, "I offered, but Dave said that he was alright and that he wouldn't drop them again."

Pierre said, "He's really stoned, and after all, it's the first time that he's smoked weed, man, and my mouth is like this desert that we're driving through."

So, David drove them the hundred miles out of his way, and before dropping them off, he gave the two of them his telephone number and address and declared that they were very welcome to call on him "the next time you're going near Albuquerque." The dudes got out of the car and together said, "Wow, just how fucking cool was that, what a laugh, that dude was totally blitzed. What a cool policeman he turned out to be and how un-fucking real was that, man?"

The dudes started hitchhiking again along Route 66. After a couple of days, they arrived in Waterbury, Connecticut. Pierre got a job with his uncle, who only had enough work for one mechanic. Patrick got a job with Pierre's two cousins in the aluminum-siding industry recovering houses. Patrick told the cousins that he had also worked as a roofer from a young age for his father, whereupon they told Patrick that they had two large houses and an apartment building that needed new roofs, so Patrick took the job on as a self-employed roofer.

Patrick and Pierre drove to Quebec one weekend to meet Pierre's family in Shawinigan Sud and spent the weekend there, visiting Montreal for the nightlife. They were driving back to the US border at the end of the weekend, and on the way, Patrick said to Pierre that he was going to have a snooze and to wake him before they reached the border so he could drive through and talk to the border guards. Pierre decided not to wake Patrick and tried to con the border checkpoint guards that he was American; they did not believe him at all because of his heavy French-Canadian accent and turned them away.

Patrick said, "Why did you not wake me up?"

Pierre replied, "I speak excellent English."

Patrick said, "I know that, but you speak with a heavy accent."

Pierre says, "Don't worry, I know another way through some back roads; we will go that way."

Patrick says, "Are you sure? I don't want to end up in jail trying to get back into my own country."

"Don't worry; it will be fine, just about half an hour detour," Pierre said. "Let's put our wigs on just in case." We took the back roads to cross the border illegally. We got across the border and were immediately followed by the border patrol and were ordered to follow them to the border police station, where we were put into a cell.

After a while of arguing with Pierre about the situation, Patrick said, "I got to get out of here had a look through the door window, which was about eight-by-eleven inches with bars but no glass."

Patrick peered through the window and noticed that the key was in the outside door lock, so Patrick sat down on the bench and untied his bootlace and pulled one lace completely out of the boot, which were US Army surplus's boots with extremely stiff leather laces. He formed a hook on one end of the lace and lowered it through the window and managed to hook the key and pull it back into the cell and unlocked the door and took his wig off, holding it in his hand, and then proceeded into the office where three officers were sitting at their desks. Patrick appeared into the room without being noticed and said to them, "What's it going to take to get out of here?"

The three simultaneously jumped out of their chairs, saying, "How in fucking hell did you get in here!?"

Patrick replied, "Don't worry about that, just tell me what will it take to get out of here."

The sergeant said, "That there is a fine totaling three hundred dollars to pay today before we can release the both of you, but you will have to take the car back to Connecticut, as it is registered there. Pierre will have to wait in the reception area here for his family to pick him up."

Patrick paid the fines, said goodbye to Pierre, and drove back to Waterbury, and that was the last time he'd see his friend Pierre.

New Year's Day 2002 and March 14, 2023 Hearing the Voice of the Lord and the Battle for Easter

It is approximately 3:00 p.m. at the Church of the Holy Sepulchre in Jerusalem, and Patrick is in a queue and is in line waiting to see the place where Jesus Christ was laid to rest and was resurrected. He is talking to a group of pilgrims consisting of four or five Chinese pilgrims from America and three or four more people from Australia, along with about six or seven other pilgrims also from America that have been on a faith tour of the Holy Land together since the tenth of March. Patrick is relating to them the events that took place starting in the living room of his house, which culminated with him being fired from his job for being a Christian.

It is New Year's Day, 2002, and he's thinking, well, that was an expensive holiday period, while pondering the thought of working over the Easter weekend, as he would have been paid an extra ninety-hour overtime. He has been working on the weekend night shifts for the past six years and had worked one Easter weekend previously. And as he was thinking about along these lines, suddenly, a voice could be heard, as if someone was standing right in front of him saying, "Pat, don't work this Easter, honor me."

Patrick says out loud, "Are you sure Lord, I can make a lot of extra money if I work, and I've just had a very expensive Christmas and New Year, my Lord. And I know that it has been said in the Bible that we should not esteem any day greater than another," but nonetheless he started to thumb through the Bible and after a little while, he says, "Okay, Lord, I've got the message, and I will put in the holiday request and honor you and your name, Lord Jesus."

Patrick is now at his place of employment, seen asking his workmates if any of them has put in a holiday request for the Easter weekend. Only one of his colleagues had put in a request for time off during the holiday weekend. The company had a policy to allow two printers off per shift. Patrick put his request in writing and submitted it to the press room manager to confirm. Nick Cole, the pressroom manager, declined the holiday request, stating that they might not have enough people available to cover his absence to allow his holiday request.

Patrick could then be heard on the phone, speaking to his boss, a Mr. Ian Gumm, the manufacturing manager, and Patrick is saying to him, "I'm a Christian, and the voice of the Lord said to me: 'Pat, don't work this Easter, honor me,' therefore I will not work this Easter weekend. I will honor the Lord."

Mr. Gumm replied, "You will work the Easter weekend."

Patrick said, "I will not work the Easter weekend, not unless you put it in writing and post a letter to arrive to me no later than Maundy Thursday, then I'll work the weekend, and when I am done, there will be no doubt that I will be giving it the shoes."

On the following Friday, Patrick can now be seen greeted by Dave, saying, "Go and get Tony Dinatale and meet me in the plate room for a meeting with myself and the plate room manager."

As it turns out, Patrick is being given a recorded verbal warning related to the phone conversation that he had with Mr. Gumm. And in particular relating to the threat of "giving it the shoes," a reference to scripture found in the New Testament, said by Jesus to the disciples as he sent them out two by two, referring to the reception their spirits had received by the people that they had witnessed to, saying, "If they receive your spirit, stay there and heal the sick, cause the blind to see and preach the gospel to them. And if they reject your spirit, shake off the dust of the shoes of your feet as a testimony against them, it will be more tolerable for Sodom and Gomorra in the day of judgement than for that place."

And following this verbal warning, there had been many confrontations with the management in the lead-up to Easter Weekend, until about two weeks before the Easter, when Patrick can be seen talking to Kevin Harding, the deputy shop steward. Kevin is telling him that there is a clause in the house agreement stating that if you can get guaranteed cover, you can have any time off whatsoever, and there's nothing the management can do to keep you from having this time off. Patrick then approached two colleagues to see if they would give him the guaranteed cover that he needed for the Easter weekend period. Andy Gooch said that he would cover Easter Sunday, and John Winter said that he would cover the Easter Saturday. And the company had already conceded that he could have Good Friday off, as they would only be running three of the presses that night.

Now on Maundy Thursday, Mr. Gumm phoned Mr. Russel Butler, the supervisor in charge of the shift that Andy Gooch and John

Winter worked under, and informed Mr. Butler that Patrick had phoned work to say that he was coming to work after all, this information being an absolute lie. Mr. Gumm then instructed Mr. Butler to cancel the guaranteed cover.

Patrick then returned to work after the Easter weekend had finished. Upon arriving at work, Mr. Grist had handed him a return-to-work form, which people would normally be receiving when returning to work after having time off because of sickness or for unauthorized time off. Patrick had also not received his weekly payroll slip. When Patrick questioned Mr. Grist as to the reason for this, Mr. Grist said that he didn't know, and he told Pat to phone Mr. Gumm on Monday.

Patrick phoned Mr. Gumm and was informed that he was not entitled to holiday pay because he had an unauthorized day off in between bank holidays; this was due to the lack of cover on the Easter Saturday night shift. Patrick then asked Andy why he had not covered his shift as agreed. Andy replied with anger and in a threatening fashion, that the management had told him that he wasn't required. John Winter had told Patrick that he also was told not to come to work as well, although he didn't believe the management, and he never believed anything that the management told him and came to work in spite of what he was told. And he stated that he had worked the entire shift on Patrick's machine and with Patrick's crew on the Saturday night in question, covering Patrick's time off and therefore negating the unauthorized day off in between bank holidays and fulfilling the BPIF's and the company's requirements.

Patrick then demanded that the company pay him for wages that they had deceitfully withheld and that they should also issue an apology for their actions. The management refused to adhere to Patrick's request. This stand that the company adopted had angered Patrick to a very large degree. Patrick then wrote a letter expressing his disappointment at their behavior and accused them of being satanically inspired by their actions against him and demanded an apology by the end of May, or he would take the matter into his own hands and deal with the situation according to his own faith.

On the following Thursday, Patrick is outside of his home looking up towards the sky, and he says, "The wind is my friend and the clouds are my friends and the rain and the thunder are my friends, Lord, send a bolt of lightning to the factory on Thursday right in the middle of the *Economist* run, while their reps are still at the site and when Annette and Ian Gumm are talking to each other in the car park, and knock out the presses and the bindery for three to three and a half hours. And then let them get the presses and bindery back online and finish the job, so that none of my friends lose their jobs by not finishing the Economist. Oh, yes, and also, my Lord, send a bolt of lightning to where Andy Gooch will be. Let the bolt of lightning be close enough to Andy so that he knows that he shouldn't have been aggressive towards me, but please Lord, as I really like Andy, and I'm sure that you do as well, don't let him be hurt in any way, in Jesus's name I pray, oh Lord."

Patrick returned to work the following day, armed with the letter he had prepared for the management with five copies, two for union officials and the rest for the senior management. Early in the shift on Friday night, David Grist, the weekend Plant Manager, approached Patrick and asked him, saying, "Why didn't you want to come to work that Easter weekend, as you have worked the Easter weekend three years previously? Why the big deal and all the arguments?"

Patrick replied that the Lord had told him not to work this Easter weekend.

Mr. Grist said, "I don't care about your religion."

Patrick said, "I don't have any religion, all I have is faith in God, the Bible, and in Jesus's name."

David retorted, "I don't care about your faith."

Patrick then told David that he would care and that he would even pray about his faith. "And now I'm going to tell you why, Dave. Yesterday, I asked the Lord to send a bolt of lightning here, to hit the factory on this coming Thursday, right in the middle of the *Economist* run, while the *Economist* reps are here, and that both Ian and Annette shall see it hit the factory while they're talking to each other outside in the car park, and they will have to wait until things are back to normal before they can go home, and it will knock out the pressroom and the bindery for three-and-a-half hours. After that, you will get everything back online and finish the *Economist* magazine on time, so that none of my friends will lose their jobs, and that means you in particular, as you are the one in charge, my friend."

When various other people on the shop floor had seen Pat having this conversation with Dave, out of curiosity they asked him, "What were you talking to Dave about?" So, he told anyone who asked him, including the two Moslem assistants that worked on his crew on press two, exactly what he had said to Dave.

Patrick is now back at the factory, the day after the lightning bolt hit the factory, as Patrick had said to David Grist and many other work colleagues the week before. Lots of different people approached

Patrick, saying, "Did you really tell all those people that this lightning thing would happen?"

Patrick replied, "Yes, I did." And nearly all of them also asked him if he could get the lottery numbers. Patrick replied, "My gift is not for the purpose of promoting the love of money and gathering worldly wealth, my gift is for the promotion of the benefit of simply being in the will of God. And to use my faith accordingly, as a sign from the Almighty, that I might gain some to be followers of Jesus!"

Patrick then came back to the factory to work a couple of overtime shifts the week after the lightning had struck the factory. It was a Tuesday day shift; Andy Gooch approached Patrick and said that he was very sorry about the way he had spoken to him, and he also told Patrick about how he and his girlfriend had been to a funfair and a bolt of lightning had hit the ground between ten and fifteen feet away from them.

Andy then said, "When the lightning hit, I knew straightaway that it was a warning from the Almighty that I shouldn't have spoken to you so aggressively like the way that I did."

Patrick replied, "That's okay, mate, the Lord forgives you, and I forgive you as well."

Andy said, "Thanks, Pat, that lightning really scared the hell out of me, mate."

Patrick replied, "I knew it would have that effect, I did ask the Lord to send that lightning, but I also asked the Lord not to let you to be hurt in any way. It says our God is a burning fire and quite a scary entity at times, but He can be very forgiving, my brother, as well."

Patrick had seen Mr. Gumm talking to some colleagues, and then Mr. Gumm approached Patrick and said that he was talking to Annette out in the car park and was just about to get into his car to go home, and then he saw the lightning hit the factory. So, he had to return to the shop floor and couldn't go home until things were sorted out. Then he said, "Did you have anything to do with that; I heard that you had told Dave Grist that all these things that happened, would happen?"

Patrick said, "I did ask the Lord to send that bolt of lightning in Jesus's name, and then it happened, exactly as I had requested from the Almighty God in heaven, dude. You can draw your own conclusions as to whether I had anything to do with that or not!"

The Beginning of the Process of Being Made Unemployed

I am reading from a handwritten note; it starts off as a file note with the heading of: "Off-the-record meeting with P. O'Malley, supervisor's office, dated the 15th of March, 2002, at 7:30 pm, present D. Grist, B. Barnes, P. O'Malley, T. Dinatale. An off-the-record meeting with P. O'MALLEY to discuss his attitude to a decision from management not to allow Pat any holidays over the Easter period due to the heavy workload at this time. It was made very clear to Pat that any threats or curses made to any individual management or otherwise would not be tolerated, and any further instances of this nature would be dealt with very severely and could invoke the disciplinary procedures under the dignity at work policy. Signed, D. Grist."

The next page that I'm about to read is a letterhead stating that Saint Ives web division St. Ives Web Limited Saint Ives house Lavington Street, London SE1 0NX, telephone: (020)7928-8844, fax: (020-7902-6393), private and confidential. Mr. P. O'Malley, 39 Whickham Highway, Dunston, Gateshead, Tyne & Wear NE11 9QJ our reference MG/JPS/P 14th of June, 2002.

"Dear Mr. O'Malley, I am writing further to my letter dated the 5th of June, 2002, and our subsequent telephone conversations. As you are aware, a complaint has been raised by Annette Remmert, Director, and general manager of Saint Ives Peterborough Limited in respect of the perceived threatening and intimidating content of the letter dated the 14th of April, 2002, which was written by you. Please find attached a copy of a letter addressed to me from Ms. Remmert setting out details of her complaint following the meeting held on the 29th of May, 2002. Both myself and Jane Broomfield Smith felt it necessary to investigate your allegations regarding the refusal of holiday leave over Easter 2002 bank holiday, as this was your main reason for sending the letter dated the 14th of April, 2002, to Annette Remmert. We will be able to advise you of our findings at the disciplinary meeting which will now take place at 12 noon on Wednesday 19th of June, 2002, in the boardroom at Saint Ives Peterborough Ltd. As already advised, you are entitled to be accompanied at the meeting by a work colleague or union representative as requested. The broad format of the meeting will be as follows: opening introductions, purpose of meetings, formalities, allegations/ complete details of complete findings of investigation to date, response by P. O'Malley to allegations, complete questions/discussions, summarise points, close the meeting for a period of adjournment to consider any action."

The next page that I'm about to read is a letter from myself to Ms. Remmert. Letters addressed to St. Ives Peterborough Ltd. Story's Bar Road, Peterborough dated the 14th of April, 2002.

"Dear Ms Remmert, I am writing this letter in order to inform you of my intention. I feel compelled to make you aware my disappointment of the treatment I received at your hands, i.e. the lack of wages paid in regard to Good Friday as you have decided to withhold payment in accordance with national agreements. I believe Good Friday falls outside of this premise to the fact that, prior to the Easter weekend, Mr. Gumm and Mr. Grist had informed me that I would not be required to work on Good Friday night. I had previously related to Mr. Gumm that I would be out of the UK from the 25th of March returning to Newcastle on Good Friday evening due to this fact, and I had also informed Mr. Gumm that I would need written notice if I was ultimately required to work the remaining shifts of the Easter weekend. I serve God, and the voice of the Lord told me not to work over the Easter weekend. I didn't ask why at the time, but I think I might know now; therefore, I also stated categorically to Mr. Gumm that if I had not received written notice that I would not be there over the Holy weekend. I handed my holiday form in in January. Mr. Cole wrote informing me that my request has been denied. I made subsequent efforts to obtain this time off for private worship and meditation during Easter; as I said before, I serve God. You seem to serve Mammon. In the light of this, I have come to this conclusion: your actions towards me have been totally unrighteous and Satanically inspired. Therefore, as a Christian and disciple of Jesus Christ, it is my godly duty to inform you that unless you repent and fully restore the wages that have been deceitfully withheld that you, Ms. Remmert, will be subject to scriptural reprisal according to the Word of God. You've chosen to degrade the cross of Christ and to devalue the cost of his sacrifice through this action of victimisation and persecution against me, a servant of Jesus Christ and the most-high God. I also feel that you have compromised my contract of employment by the decision that you have made in the past, i.e. to suspend me off the sick scheme on numerous occasions the rules state that employees could be suspended if they abuse the sick scheme. I have not abused the sick scheme at all; laws and rules made by people are subject to scrutiny. The laws of God are infallible and are upheld by love, faith, and righteousness; your judgement followed by your actions in the past are an insult to me in spirit, and your action regarding the Easter weekend is an insult to Christ. These are not the only insults that need considering; I am referring to an alleged statement made by yourself and the late Mr. Trapmore sometime in late August 1999. If you recall to memory regarding the manipulation of the wages clerk to obtain funds while I was attending my gravely ill father in Arizona, USA, something you have already denied in an earlier confrontation, although I still have my doubts. When I started work at St. Ives in September 1996, I asked the Lord to bless this company and make it prosperous. Since then I have had numerous reasons to ask the Lord to remove that blessing and turn it into a curse; if I continue to receive this unacceptable treatment of disrespecting contempt and do not receive a full apology and the restitution of all funds that are been deceitfully withheld by you in good faith by the end of May, then I will have no other option but to invoke the holy Scriptures of God in the name of Jesus Christ according to my faith. I must confess that I am disappointed that you have chosen to make yourself an adversary and had not rather chosen a more congenial path of perception in your judgement regarding me; the Lord has promised me that He will avenge me of all my enemies, as the Scripture says, after the first or second admonishment. Therefore, you can consider this letter to be your first admonishment in the word.

Yours faithfully in Jesus Christ, signed P. L. O' Malley.

Southern Print 2003

Malcom is now watching Patrick as he starts working at Southern Print in Poole, County Dorset. And after ten months have passed, the union branch secretary comes to the factory and approaches him and asks him if he is Patrick O'Malley. He replies "Yes, I am." The man then asked him if he was the same man that got fired from St. Ives for being a Christian? Patrick replies, "Yes."

The man then asked, "Is it true that you had prophesied that a bolt of lightning would hit the factory and then it happened?"

Patrick replied, "Yes."

The man then stuck out his hand and said, "I'm very pleased to meet you. And I will do as much as I can on your behalf. I have been informed by your Chapel representatives that you have been working here on a temporary contract and that you have applied for a permanent position after having been asked by all four supervisors and by the print manager if you would consider staying on as a full-time employee, is that correct?"

Patrick replied, "Yes that is correct. Well, what has happened since?"

The print manager told me that he had sent an email to the managing director notifying him of his intention to formally offer a permanent position, and then the managing director had told him that he had spoken to someone at St. Ives, Peterborough, and after having a conversation with someone unknown to me, that there is no way that he would approve this offer of employment. This was after Brian had said to me that he was trying to save my job.

I said to him, “What do you mean, you yourself have made the job offer on two separate occasions?”

Then Brian said that his mother was also a committed Christian as well and that he really felt terrible and gutted by this unfortunate situation and was very sorry, but it was now out of his hands.

December 19, 2004: Gateshead Magistrate Court: Enemies, Perhaps Not

When Patrick had vacated his flat in Poole and had returned to his home in the northeast, he phoned St. Ives to inform them that since they had broken the agreement drawn up by ACAS, that he now had the right to also inform them that he would now invoke the scriptures that he had made them aware of, and this would be the last time that he would speak with them about this issue. The St. Ives Group took Patrick to court as a result of that phone call, and they sent a barrister and a solicitor to Gateshead Magistrates. After having terminated Patrick's contract of employment because they felt threatened and intimidated by his presence, whereof they accused him of having special powers because of the lightning and the common knowledge within the factory about the lightning that Patrick had prophesied to Mr. Grist and other colleagues on the shop floor.

The day before the the court hearing, Patrick phoned the court and asked if he could bring his son with him. The court replied, yes that shouldn't be a problem. When we prepared to enter the courtroom, we were told that the judge had decided that the case would be a closed hearing and therefore no one else would be permitted into the courtroom. Yet earlier on the way to the courthouse, Chris said, So they are sending a solicitor and a barrister and you're on your own. So what are you going to do pappy? He said, son, I'm going to do what the Bible says. Chris says, so what is that? He said, it basically says, not to think about what you're going to say, because I will give you a mouth that speaks words of wisdom that they will neither be able to gain say nor resist. And I will win the case and they will have to pay for it.

The barrister approached Patrick in the waiting room saying, "Are you Patrick O'Malley?"

Patrick replied "Yes, are you my enemy?"

The man replied, "No."

Patrick said, "Are you trying to put me in jail?"

The barrister replied, "Yes."

Patrick then said to him, "Well, then you must be my enemy; after all, a friend wouldn't endeavor to imprison his friend, would he?"

They then entered the courtroom to hear the judge deliberate. Approximately forty minutes later, the judge called for a recess. And while they were in the lobby of the courtroom, Patrick said to the barrister, "Do you know about the lightning that hit the factory?"

The barrister replied "Yes, I know everything about this case, including the lightning strike that hit the factory."

Patrick then told the man that he had asked the Lord to send that bolt of lightning in Jesus's name and then it happened. "And you want to be my enemy."

At this point, the barrister lost his composure and replied, "It's just a fucking job, I don't want to be your enemy."

Patrick said, "Okay, dude, calm down, I don't blame you, if I was someone else other than myself, I wouldn't want to be my enemy either, that would be a scary thing knowing that there is no doubt that

God is with me and has anointed and seated me according to His will and pleasure."

The three then reentered the courtroom. The judge, Mr. Ray Watson, had a stack of paperwork in front of him, about a hundred pages of content about Patrick, the things that happened at the factory, and other things related to Patrick that they had included in their testimony. The judge had said that he had read all this testimony last night, and after reading this, he couldn't get to sleep, as all this very unusual evidence that he had read about Patrick played on his mind, and then he said, "I suppose that you couldn't get to sleep either."

Patrick replied, "I didn't have any problem with getting to sleep, as I have known all those things written about me all my life, even before they happened, ever since the Lord decided to bless me with His anointing."

The judge ruled in Patrick's favor, stating that no threat had been made and that there was no reason to support the harassment accusation. And provided Patrick with the concession to enable him to write to certain St. Ives employees, which he did.

The Friends

Suddenly the vision changed from the courtroom appearance, and the viewpoint was from a very different perspective. Patrick said to Malcom, "These are my friends: spiritual beings, angels, and cherubs yielding fiery swords, accompanied with prophets of old, the disciples of Christ, and a host of the followers of Jesus with the light of their Lord all around them. Patrick said that these are my friends and yours too and anybody else's that would desire it to be so, my friend."

August 1996: Summer Rain? A Roofer's Paradise

Malcom then observed Patrick talking on the phone with his brother Dennis, DJ, as he had always been called by Patrick, and the rest of the family, and DJ was asking Patrick if he would ask the Lord to send a rainstorm to Phoenix because it hadn't rained in the area for some time. DJ needed to make some money for his mortgage payment, as he is a self-employed roofer. Patrick replied that the Lord wasn't going to send any rain, although He would send a windstorm.

DJ said, "Wind is okay, but the rain will get the people to realize that their roofs leak, so could you just ask Him to send a rainstorm?"

Patrick said, "I will ask Him, but I don't believe that the Lord is going to send a rainstorm just now. There will be a time in the future when I will ask the Lord to send a storm to Arizona that will be described as impossible, and yet the impossible will happen!"

Four or five days had expired, and DJ phoned his brother again, this time complaining that Patrick hadn't asked the Lord to send the rain. Patrick said, "I did ask the Lord to send the rain, but I knew that the Lord didn't want to send rain, but He would send a mighty wind."

At this point DJ said, "Wind is okay, but you still need rain so that the people would know that their roofs leaked."

Patrick said, "Don't worry about the rain, this windstorm is going to be a mighty wind of desolation, a judgment and a sign from the Almighty. And some rain will accompany the windstorm, but even without any rain, there will be enough work for you and every other roofer in Arizona, plus thousands of other roofers from other nearby states. And you and the thousands of other roofers will have enough work to last for at least a year."

This windstorm did happen within a few days of the conversation that they had. And it took over a year for the roofers of Arizona and the thousands of other roofers from outside of the state to repair the roof damage sustained in that windstorm. And every time that Patrick went to visit his family in Arizona, DJ would introduce him to some of his friends and say, "This is my brother, and the dude that I told you about, and that mega windstorm that he asked the Lord to send."

Patrick was reminiscing in the past when he was just fourteen years old and DJ was thirteen, back when their dad would drive them to Sunset Beach to surf the inside point, where nobody else surfed because of the rocky shoreline and before the invention of the ankle leash. Neither of them had ever lost their board to the rocks, even though they had surfed there all summer and the following summer as well.

One day when the waves were very moderate, I watched DJ attempt a fin first take off and somehow pulling it off on the first attempt. I was flabbergasted as he rode it out nose first. Then the laughter started as he repeated the manoeuvre and fell off over and over again and I thought that that goofy footer brother of mine was a funny guy after all. And eventually he made that manoeuvre his own.

Early 1972: Meeting the Children of God Group

Patrick as now being observed by Malcom walking on the pier located at Pismo Beach, California; he is with Paul, a friend from Connecticut. It's late morning, and the two of them are watching and listening to a young man playing Patrick's acoustic guitar. Moments after, the young man finishes playing and hands the guitar back to Patrick with bleeding fingers from the steel strings on the guitar. Patrick had been mesmerized by his playing, just as a bunch of young people singing and dancing towards him surrounded Patrick and his friends, still singing and dancing around them. Patrick was really enjoying the atmosphere that they had created and ended up following them to their very large marquee about a mile down from the beach. Then he ended up staying with them at the beach for the rest of the day and stayed that night.

These people turned out to be the Christian cult group known as the Children of God, whose infamous founder and leader was a Mr. David Berg. He would write epistles to various colonies dotted around the world. He called these epistles "Mo Letters" after his self-imbued biblical name of Moses David.

Patrick had joined their group and was renamed Jabbok Otob. And as it turned out, this was the only thing that they had in common; that is to say, Moses David, up until that time, and Jabbok Otob were the only two males that had two different names. All the other disciples that were recruited were renamed with just one biblical name. The new recruits were taken to a mountainous region in Northern California for the purpose of studying the Bible and to memorize a standard set of scriptures that would help with witnessing to potential Christians, whom might be ready to be born again and possibly become candidates to join the Children of God group.

After about six weeks of training, the babes, as they were called at the time, were taken out into the general public to witness their newfound faith to the world, giving the message of hope in Jesus to a new generation, consisting of the hippie movement. This also included Patrick is one of many in that 60s hippies movement.

He was then sent to the Santa Barbara colony for a couple of weeks, where the colony's leader had renamed Patrick in the first instance, Jabbok Otob, saying to him, "We usually give one biblical name to new recruits, but with a name like yours, Patrick O'Malley, I just love your name, so as far as I'm concerned, you just have to have a second name."

Patrick was then sent to the Fresno colony, where he learned American Sign Language and got baptized in a Yosemite mountain lake. After being baptized and returning to the colony, after a few days, he receives the vision from the Lord that he can never forget and the greatest evidence of salvation, seeing his name written in the book of life and being reassured by the voice of Jesus to follow him and fear no more. Patrick then moved on to another colony located in Portland, Oregon. After a couple of days, he informed one of the colony's elders that he was a draft dodger and that he was also wrongly accused of car theft in Hartford, Connecticut, supposedly stealing a car in the state of Maine, where he had never been before, and then transporting it to

Connecticut. Some of the elders advised him to go back to Connecticut and turn himself into the authorities there. The next day one of the elders drove Patrick to the highway about thirty miles due east of Portland, Oregon, and dropped him off to hitchhike.

Early 1972: Fresno, California, Dreams and Visions

Patrick is now being observed as a young man again in a house, another colony of the Children of God in Fresno, California; he is in a bedroom by himself on his hands and knees, praying to the Almighty, after having had a very scary dream of being on the edge of a bottomless pit, glowing with the embers of hell, the night before. Malcom is now watching Patrick together with Patrick himself, as they both are observing his spirit as it rises from his body while praying. His spirit appears as a luminous shade of a blue representation of his physical body. And it appears to both until the apparition disappears as it reaches the ceiling, although the vision of what Patrick and Malcolm see continues. He is now in a place that looks like the wilderness, and he's not aware of his body anymore. He sees the wilderness and states how beautiful the place is to a presence that is beside him in this spiritual wilderness, as the companion next to him says, "Yes, it is," and then tells him to continue to go forward.

He moves forward until, suddenly, he reaches what looks like a wall of bright, clear, blue sky in front, above, and below, and to his left and his right, nothing else but this bright, clear, blue wall of sky. At this point, Patrick stops moving forward. The companion next to him tells him that he should not be afraid, but he should rather go forward. Patrick then moves forward, and instantly the sky changes from the bright blue as it first appeared into near blackness. And although in the darkness and in the distance, there can be seen a circular shape outlined in the darkness with the color of it being a shade of dark sapphire as it appears in the background. Whereupon there could be seen white lights that were emerging from its center and apparently moving towards Patrick, all of them being the same shape and brightness but differing in size, resembling the human form but consisting only of light-bearing energy.

Patrick showed amazement at seeing these celestial beings until he noticed the large sapphire sphere from which the beings of light had appeared, itself becoming larger and brighter. The sapphire sphere itself started to become brighter and changed its color until it morphed into a very bright shade of amber. At this point, Patrick went down on his knees and closed his eyes in fear. And immediately, he heard the voice beside him saying, "Don't be afraid, open your eyes," which he did. The voice then asked, "What do you see?"

Patrick replied, "I see a large, white, stone block with a big, black book on it."

The voice then said, "Open the book," so he opened the book. The voice then said, "What do you see?"

Patrick replied, "I see my full given name written in it."

The voice then said, "Don't be afraid, for your name is written in the book of life."

Then I saw Patrick's spirit return to his body, and he arose, changed from what he had been into a man without the fear of damnation and because of his confidence in that same voice that accompanied him throughout his life's journey.

Hitchhiking to Hell's Kitchen

After leaving Portland, Patrick hitchhiked for a while until a highway patrol policeman stopped and made him aware of the law forbidding the act of hitchhiking in the state of Oregon, also issuing a citation for breaking the law. After the police officer left, Patrick resumed hitch-hiking until a Chevy El Camino stopped and offered him a ride. This slightly older couple told him that he would have to ride in the back of the El Camino; Patrick replied, "That's cool, thanks."

After driving for a good hundred and fifty miles, they pulled into a roadside cafe. The man said that they were going to have something to eat. "You're welcome to join us."

Patrick thanked him and got out of the vehicle and went into the cafe with the couple. The man offered to buy Patrick a meal, which he graciously accepted.

The three of them had a conversation over dinner, and the couple explained that they were Christians and asked Patrick for his point of view on this subject. Patrick then told them that he too is also a born-again Christian. They discussed the subject and agreed in the faith. The man said that they were going to be driving right through the night, and he was welcome to come along with them until they had reached their destination.

Patrick accepted the offer and climbed into the back of the vehicle and pulled his sleeping bag over his body and watched the stars. After a while, Patrick noticed a lightning storm taking place to the north of him, over the top of the mountain range and thought, *wow, how cool is that*; it seemed to go on for hours, like chain lightning. Patrick fell asleep and awoke in the morning when the couple had reached their turn-off on the highway. They said their goodbyes and Patrick started hitchhiking again.

Patrick got another ride within a short amount of time. The driver was a male of about twenty-five years old. He told Patrick that he had been camping in the mountains alone for approximately six weeks, as he had felt that he needed to get away from society because he had felt oppressed by civilization. He had also stated that he had no intention of leaving the mountain but somehow felt very compelled to do so. Patrick had felt a lot of compassion and empathy for this man and told him about himself and his conversion to his modern outlook on Christianity.

After quite a few hundred miles, another hitchhiker appeared on the horizon. Patrick said to the driver that he should pick him up, as he was sure that he was going to be another Children of God member. They picked up the hitchhiker, and he turned out to be another member of the Children of God sect. Not only was he a "brother," he was also the biological brother of a young woman named Phyllis, whom had been a girlfriend of Patrick six months earlier when he was living in Connecticut. He was also travelling to Connecticut to join the colony in Hartford.

Patrick arrived in Hartford at the Children of God colony in the afternoon and told the elders of his situation concerning the police and the draft board. The elders or colony leaders said that as far as they are concerned, he is no longer Patrick O'Malley, so therefore they advised that Jabbok Otob should not report to the Hartford police or get in touch with the draft board, but rather than that, he should travel to the colony situated in Hell's Kitchen, New York City, and from there he should leave the United States and go to another colony abroad.

Jabbok Otob made his way to New York City and reported to the Hell's Kitchen Children of God colony. The leaders sent him to the airport to get a standby ticket to London, but while there, for some unknown reason, a boil had developed on his right foot. It was so severely awkward and painful that he couldn't walk more than a few feet at a time and was stuck at the airport with one of the members of the Hell's Kitchen colony. They were at the airport for roughly forty hours, by which time the Children of God brother telephoned the colony and asked for advice.

They told him that they were going to come to the airport and pick up the two of them. "Jabbok Otob will have to stay at the colony until he's able to walk, even though he needs to get out of the country as quickly as possible. This brother, Jabbok Otob, is not going to Vietnam, and we all know that he is innocent of the alleged car theft, as he has never even been in the state of Maine before."

Jabbok Otob stayed at the colony for about seven weeks and eventually joined a group of about twenty members of the Children of God that had gotten together from different parts of America and boarded a flight to London, England.

August 1st 1972: Leaving the USA for London

While Jabbok Otob was staying with the Children of God in England, he studied the Bible wholeheartedly. He also studied the "Mo Letters." And until that point, Jabbok Otob's contribution to the group was to work with the mechanical team, repairing their various vehicles; he even spent his twenty-first birthday under a double-decker, topless touring bus, replacing the clutch assembly for the group.

Jabbok Otob started categorizing the Mo Letters' context for himself so that he could quote relevant content to the people that he would be witnessing to concerning the life of faith in God. The Children of God leadership got to know what Jabbok Otob was doing and approached him for his ideas.

Jabbok Otob suggested that they should create an index for the greater use of the membership. He was then seconded into the index team that was created from his suggestion. He stayed with the team until the index was nearly finished. That is until the day that he had related some Bible scriptures that the Lord had told him to give to Faith, the daughter of David Berg, known as, Moses-David, the self-professed Prophet of God, proclaimed by himself and other-wisely known as "The Branch."

Within a few days upon receiving the set of scriptures, Jabbok Otob was dismissed from the index team, moved out of headquarters, and put into the print shop for retraining, where he took residence in the flat above the converted row of garages, which had formerly been stables. Within four to six weeks, Jabbok Otob printed the finished index for the Children of God group.

In this time, Jabbok Otob met Magdalene. These two got married within the group at a Children of God ceremony. Suddenly a new Mo Letter called "The Flirty Little Fishes" appeared in the headquarters colony in the autumn of 1973, where they now lived, at Tavistock Street in Covent Garden, in the Westend of London, England.

Within a few days of reading the new Mo Letter, Jabbok Otob had told his wife that there was no way that he was going to print this new Mo Letter and send it out to the other communes dotted around the world. Patrick and his newlywed wife, Magdalene, left the Children of God cult group immediately and permanently. This was long before they renamed the group "The Family." And the two of them hitchhiked northward on the motorway out of London and got dropped off at the Luton underpass, where he had asked the good Lord to create an umbrella of grace.

Early 1974: The Referee

Before Patrick and June got legally married, they travelled to Hartlepool to spread the gospel on quite a few different occasions and eventually decided to move there after making some good friends on their visits. Patrick got on particularly well with Colin and his best mate Sugar. After having lived there for a while, Colin and Sugar asked Patrick if he and June fancied going for a swim at the baths.

Patrick replied, "Aren't they closed; It's, like, nearly ten o'clock."

Sugar said, "That's not a problem; I used to work there, and I have a set of keys for the whole complex."

Patrick replied, "Sure, dude, that's cool."

Later that night after the swim, Colin said, "How would you and June like to come to a Sunday league match tomorrow to watch Sugar and I play for our team?"

Patrick replied, "Sure, dude, that's cool with me; what about you, sweetheart, do you fancy going?"

June says, "Aye, why not."

The next morning, June and Patrick met the lads on the football pitches. After greeting the lads, Patrick and June stood at the side of the pitch waiting for the game to start. They had waited for a good ten to fifteen minutes when Colin and the captain of the other team approached Patrick and said, "The referee hasn't turned up and since you're the only bloke around here, would you referee the game?"

Patrick said, "Are you crazy? I don't know anything whatsoever about soccer; we never played it in California when I was growing up, so how could I even begin to referee the game, are you guys nuts?"

Colin and the other dude said, "Well, just try to follow the ball as it moves from player to player; it's okay, mate. We'll tell you when to blow the whistle and when a foul is committed and what to do in relation to the foul."

Patrick replied, "Okay, but I can see that this could be what you dudes call dodgy!"

The game started and was going well without a problem for the first twenty minutes, when Patrick was told by Colin to blow the whistle for a penalty kick. There followed a lot of upheaval about the decision, but Patrick stood by Colin and Sugar's insistence that the foul was genuine. The penalty attempt shot missed the goalmouth completely. The game continued with a few free kicks being awarded by the ref for another fifteen minutes or so until Colin shouted to Patrick that another penalty foul had been committed, to which there was a lot of disputation, yet again. But like the first penalty call, Patrick stood by his friend's judgment and awarded the penalty kick; this time, the penalty taker made no mistake and put the ball into the back of the net.

The game continued for another few minutes when Colin and Sugar approached Patrick and said, "Look, we've overheard some of the other team members saying that they were going to fill us in at halftime." Colin continued, "When it gets closer to halftime, Sugar and I will make our way to the corner flag; when you see us over in the corner, start coming towards us and blow the halftime whistle when you are close to us, when we signal to you, then follow us, as we know this area very well, and they haven't got a clue about the area, so we should be able to lose them pretty quickly."

As it approached halftime, true to their word, Colin and Sugar were at the corner waiting for Patrick to blow the halftime whistle, and while looking at them giving the heads up, Patrick blew the whistle and ran like a gazelle, following Colin and Sugar, jumping hedges and small fences with the whole of the opposing team in hot pursuit. After a couple of hundred meters or so, we had totally lost our pursuers. From there we went to Colin's flat, and after catching our breath, we all had one hell of a laugh, with Colin and Sugar saying, "Wow, those two penalty calls really pissed them off," howling with laughter and saying, "Cheers, mate, you played a belter, we knew you had it in you to be a damned good referee." Patrick howled again with laughter. Patrick then asked them if those penalties were genuine penalties. They both replied, "No, not really," then Colin said, "But what the hell, mate, it was well worth the laugh. What a story, everyone that we tell this to will laugh their heads off"

After a few months, June and Patrick moved to Gateshead, where June fell pregnant. Patrick then started working as an auto mechanic for a short time, a couple of months anyway, until he got a better paying job as a roofer. He did this job until Christopher was six months old. The family then moved to California in May 1975.

Nineteen Eighties Factory Life: 1988 & '89

Malcom then observed Patrick having a conversation with two colleagues, Michael Clayton and Paul Thurston, who were both supervising print production and working in an award-winning web printing company called Hunter Print in Peterlee Co. Durham.

The print manager approached the three men and pushed Patrick towards the door saying, "Get out of this office."

Patrick hit his shoulder on the doorframe, which was made of steel, supporting the glass office. Patrick descended the staircase and reached his machine and his co-pressman, Derek Cole, who had earlier had a conversation with Patrick, stating that he didn't believe in Jesus and that he was the ultimate skeptic concerning faith in God, but was very open to discussion about that subject, and had asked Patrick, what he wanted him to tell him is that, "What would Jesus say and do about any particular issue that I want to know about?" After much deliberation, Patrick thought, *Wow, this requires a gigantic leap of faith on my part and a mountain of responsibility to try to fulfill such a request as this. For who could know the mind of God, so Lord, I will leave this up to you and your will. But I would love to persuade Derek to the point where one day I will hear him say, I believe, I believe!*

Then Derek carried on to Patrick, when observing what had happened upstairs in the glass office and said, "What was that about, and is it time for the shoes?"

Patrick replied, "Yes," and went back upstairs to the glass office and took his shoes off and shook the dust off them, saying, "Vengeance is mine, says the Lord, I will repay, and you will understand this!"

Patrick then returned to his press and started looking at the proofs and checking the copy. Patrick noticed that his two fellow printers, Derek and Bob McGill, had taken off as they saw the print manager, Peter Leach, a tall man of six foot, ten inches, approaching the press area. Mr. Leach shadowed Patrick very closely, looking down and snickering and chuckling but not saying a word, then he left.

When Derek and Bob returned, Derek says to Patrick, "What was that about, and what was he laughing at?"

Patrick said, "He thought that he was laughing at me, but he was laughing at the way the Holy Spirit had moved me to give it the shoes."

Derek said, "What's going to happen to him?"

Patrick said, "He's not going to be able to talk or laugh, he's going to be very short of breath, and he's going to go to the hospital for six weeks, laying on his back, taking short breaths during that time, and then he is going to get better, and he's going to come back to work, and then he's going to find out that I told you that these things were going to happen to him. And then, my friend, his whole life is going to change."

Some time passed, and Derek said to Patrick, "Hey, dude, I haven't seen Mr. Leach for ages."

Patrick said, "I haven't, either."

Derek said, "I'm going to find out what happened," and walked away from the press to make his enquiry. Derek returned with Mike Newbould, the press room supervisor.

Mr. Newbould said to Patrick, "Mr. Leach is in hospital; he can't speak, and he can barely breathe."

Patrick said, "Don't worry, he's going to get better, and he will be able to come back to work soon."

There is a union meeting taking place in the factory platemaking room because the FOC and his deputy found out about the company's plans to shut down the Eastleigh and Peterlee factories and to create a more centralized location in Corby, Northampton. So, they immediately got alternative local employment and left the Chapel without senior union representation. Subsequently, a union meeting took place, and one of the lads nominated Patrick to be the FOC. Several other men seconded the nomination. Patrick stood up and said that he would be their shop steward, "only if every one of you here puts your hand up," which they did to a man, about sixty-five people in total. The next thing that happened was a meeting between the new FOC and his deputy, with the management, i.e. Mr. Leach and Mr. Newbould. Mr. Leach stated that he would like to have an off-the-record meeting first. Patrick agreed; Mr. Leach stated that he had heard from colleagues that Patrick knew what had happened to him before the illness had occurred in his body.

Patrick replied, "That is true."

Mr. Leach then asked why this had happened to him. Patrick reminded him of the incident that happened in the glass office and later the shop floor, explaining to Mr. Leach that what he had witnessed with the shoes. "You subsequently laughing and snickering on the shop floor was the reason why these things happened to you. Because the Holy Spirit of God had moved me to do and say what I said. And the Holy Spirit took exception to your attitude of what you perceived as humorous. And Derek Cole asked me after witnessing these interactions and said to me, 'what's going to happen to him?' So, I told him that the scripture says God is not to be mocked, and therefore I told him what was going to happen to you, Mr. Leach."

Mr. Leach then said, "Can you ask the Lord to heal me and to help me?"

Patrick replied, "I certainly will," and immediately Patrick asked the Lord out loud to forgive and to heal Mr. Leach and to help him. Peter Leach thanked him for asking the Lord to forgive him and to help him. And then they went ahead with their meeting about the alternative options available concerning redundancies and the option of relocation on offer to the entire workforce.

About eighteen months later, Hunter Print shares dropped from an all-time high at the time of the shoes to a few pence, after the move to Northamptonshire, where the owner Mr. Michael Hunter got voted off the board and got fired along with his second-in-command, Mr. Ian Gray, just as Patrick had told Michael Clayton and Paul Thurston and relayed this information to Derek as well. Michael and Paul freaked out after the shoes and summoned Patrick to the private supervisor's office that was situated downstairs and partially below the glass office and said that they didn't want anything to do with the shoes, when Patrick replied, "Don't worry, this is not about you guys, this is about Peter Leach, the owner, and that man Ian Gray and mainly about this company and its future."

Patrick had phoned Derek shortly after these things, relating to Michael Hunter and Ian Gray and the company shares that had happened, to inquire of Derek about the availability of any jobs that he might be aware of. Derek answered the phone and upon hearing Patrick's voice, said, "I believe, I believe!" which brought joy to Patrick's heart.

PART TWO

The Reanimation of Malcom

Early June 1987: The Vortex and Black Monday

Patrick is talking to Lynn Hopper, a friend and neighbor who has been typing some of his lyrics for him. Patrick had previously written a letter, posted to Reuter's, News International, and other news outlets, stating that the Lord was going to send a wind of desolation into the midst of their indiscretion, and that being their unholy worship of the love of money and their unholy temples of worship, their beloved stock exchange and all of their temples of unholy worship shall be spoiled in Jesus's name.

Patrick then told Lynn that when he heard that the ship, *The Herald of Free Enterprise*, was to be refitted and relaunched, he had asked the Lord to send a vortex, like a hurricane but not a hurricane, that was going to come from the Atlantic and make its way into the Channel. And along the way it would cause the ship, *The Herald of Free Enterprise*, to break free of the tugboats that are towing it, and it shall not be refitted and refloated. Then the storm shall break land and then will travel through the stockbroker belt and then through into London. It will make its way into the financial sector. It will hit the building where the stock market is housed, damaging the building. Because of this, the stock market will close the day after. When the market opens again on Monday in London, that is when the crash will start, first in London, and then it will reach unto every one of their unholy temples of worship, and they will not even know why or how this crash has happened because this is a judgment and sign from the Lord.

Some months later, Patrick is now in a pub with Lynn Hopper. Lynn says, “Have you seen the news, that vortex you were talking about?”

Patrick replied, “Yes, I have, the storm the vortex carried will do what I told you it would a couple of months ago and close down the stock exchange for repairs. When they reopen on Monday, then the hand of the Holy Spirit will have His way with their false god, the love of money. And they shall know this to be a judgment from God in Jesus’s name.”

The media christened that day as Black Monday.

March 17, 1988, Apartheid; March 11, 2023, Apartheid

It is March 11, and Patrick is in Israel at the ruins of Caesarea, talking to a couple of Christian pilgrims that are on the same faith tour as him; he is talking about the letter that he wrote on March 17, 1988, to President Reagan and to Margret Thatcher, when one of the American pilgrims comes over, stands next to him, and asks the tour guide, who was also standing next to Patrick, if she would be able to buy a souvenir relating to Netanyahu, something like a comic book or an action figure for her sister, as she had heard that he was a hero.

Patrick said, "Wow, you must be joking; that man is not a hero; he is a bloodthirsty monster and a warmonger and also a total disgrace to the Jewish faith, who will not be satisfied until he has every Palestinian, man, woman, and child murdered by his diabolical system of apartheid, which is worse than South Africa was in the 1980s, and he is in the same league as Putin, both of them thinking that they have a God-given right to disobey the commandments, in particular the one that says 'thou shall not kill'! These two monsters are the perfect candidates to be at the forefront of those to be thrown into the lake of fire that burns forever and ever throughout all eternity! They and 95 percent of all the politicians in the world, who in my opinion are just another demon walking, possessed by hatred and influenced by the love of money, the root of all evil, and therefore influenced by the devil himself—all being liars!

Then Patrick continues to tell the others about the letter that he gave to Lynn Hopper to type for him, accusing America and Great Britain of hypocrisy in the stance that they have taken supporting South Africa and not condemning them for their use of apartheid and for not imposing sanctions against them. Patrick warns the United States President Ronald Reagan in a letter he composed the night before, posted on March 18, 1988, to the White House, with a copy to 10 Downing Street, and a copy sent to Desmond Tutu via Durham Cathedral during his visit to the cathedral, that the Lord is going to send a drought upon the Great Plains and upon the harvest of wheat and corn in the United States. Because the president's hypocrisy had influenced him and as he decided to invade Panama because of the sins of one man, namely Noriega, for drug trafficking offenses and do absolutely nothing about the South African sins of apartheid. Patrick warns Margret Thatcher in the same letter that unless she changes her stance on apartheid, the Lord would send flooding upon the eastern coast of the United Kingdom and upon their great city of merchandise. This letter was dated March 17, 1988. Ronald Reagan took no heed from this warning and did absolutely nothing about apartheid. Therefore, the prophesy was fulfilled, bringing a drought that destroyed the harvest even before the second curse was due to strike the United Kingdom. Margaret Thatcher changed tactics and imposed measures against South Africa, thereby avoiding the curse that the Lord had prepared for Great Britain.

March 14, 2023, and March 17, 2023

In Jericho, the Catholic faith tour went to another coffee shop with a big souvenir shop attached to it. And I was thinking, *Not again, I thought that this was a faith pilgrimage, but it's more like the time that Jesus overthrew the money changers' tables,* and he got a bit angry about this, and then he went outside and asked the Lord to bring a storm with enough rainfall to influence and expedite the need to get out of the shop. Within two minutes, it started to rain so hard that the tour guide and coach driver rounded up the people and reversed the coach to below the overhang at the back of the shop that was about ten to twelve feet in depth, and they had everybody board the coach as quickly as possible from the rear door of the coach. Everybody did board the coach as quickly as they could. And with everyone on the coach, within ten minutes we were at the bottom of the hill, driving through the water that was close to two feet high. And we left Jericho as quickly as possible, and we didn't even visit the ruins, as the rainfall was so extreme.

After Masada, March 17, 2023

The day after having visited Masada and the Dead Sea, Patrick prepared his luggage to go back home. He left the hotel on foot, and within two minutes, he came across a policeman and asked him where the Russian church was. The policeman asked Patrick if he wanted to go to the church or to the prison. He replied, "The church," and then walked to the Russian Basilica to see if he could talk to the bishop about the blessing that the church had given to the Russian army's war on Ukraine, but he was turned back by the sister who was on attendance at opening time and told to come back later that afternoon. So, he told her that he would be flying back to the United Kingdom before lunchtime. She continued that she couldn't do anything now. The church was right next to a prison where a lot of Palestinians were being held without trial, so he walked down the street for about fifty meters and sat down on a concrete bollard, thinking, *I can kill two birds with one stone here,* and he took off his shoes, shook the dust off his feet, and said, "'Vengeance is mine,' says the Lord, 'I will repay,' and you know what to do, my Lord," and then walked back to his hotel five minutes away by foot. He then got his carry-on, took a taxi to Ben Gurion airport, and flew back to the UK.

Early January 1987

Patrick is in bed; he wakes up and immediately turns the bedside light on, grabs his notebook, and starts writing. He's writing very quickly and does not stop to pause but continues until he's finished the lyrical piece that he calls "Warrior"; when he puts his pencil down, he is shaking and soaking wet with sweat and tears running down his face saying, "Now that was weird, Lord," and then he put his head down and went back to sleep.

Patrick is now at his place of employment, and he is sharing his lyrical prose with some of his colleagues. Robert McDermot returns with the piece, "Warrior," saying, "Patrick, I understood all of this except for this part, what does this mean? 'Warrior in the world lift up the staff give honour to His name, this new thing I do, summer in winter light in the shade, snow in the desert on Christmas Day,' what does this mean?"

Patrick replied, "Well, dude, the staff is like the staff of Moses; it is actually the bread of life, which is the Word of God, it feeds the spirit. Summer in winter means that this winter on Christmas Day, there will be summer weather conditions in the northern hemisphere in places like Moscow, where they will have an average summer day's temperature, and on the other hand, there will be snow in the desert in places like southern Arizona, where it's normally quite hot. The light in the shade refers to the enlightenment that the grace of God will pour upon mankind from that moment on. Now this phenomenon will happen this Christmas; Robert, this is a sign from God so that His children will be able to fully comprehend faith, my friend."

Palm Sunday 2004: You Choose, Lord

Malcom is now watching Patrick and his wife, June, at the foot of the Tor of Glastonbury.

Patrick says, "Shall we go to the top, sweetheart?"

June says, "Yes, why not?"

So, they set off together, and when they got to just over halfway, June said, "This is a bit too much for me, I will sit here on this small bench while you carry on."

Patrick said, "Okay, I won't be too long."

Patrick carried on up to the top and sat down just outside of the chapel. Patrick then put forward his supplication unto the Lord, saying, "Oh, Lord in heaven, in my own eyes and in the eyes of people that really know me, I am not seen, even by myself, as a holy man, but just a man with so many faults as any other human; if I am truly your anointed man of God, let there be three doves in the chapel and have them appear before me and then let them fly off into the sky straightaway, in Jesus's name, Amen."

Patrick then went into the chapel and immediately saw two doves perched upon the wall before him, and they flew off straightaway. Patrick then said, "I don't see the third dove, oh Lord," and as soon as he had said that, a third dove appeared right above his head and also flew off straightaway. Patrick then went outside through the other door and said, "Oh Lord, if I am your man for the latter rain, then bring me the Holy Grail up through the earth where I place my hand." Patrick looked around at the grass and placed his right hand on the ground and left it there for five to ten minutes. When he lifted his hand, he found a palm leaf shaped like a cross from Palm Sunday; that same day was Palm Sunday. Patrick picked it up and said, “Of course, the Holy Grail is a spiritual blessing and anointing and not just a physical cup, hallelujah, thank you, Lord.”

Mid-1990s and a Visit From the Jehovah's Witnesses

One day there was a knock on Patrick's front door; it was four members of the Jehovah's Witnesses, including one of Patrick's son's friends, one Sebastian Walmsley-McCarthy. Patrick was at home on his own; his wife refused to entertain any representatives of religion, especially Mormons and Jehovah's Witnesses. Patrick had a totally different view and would invite them in if they knocked when June wasn't home, as she would scream obscenities at them and would be telling them to fuck off! Patrick was differently composed and relished the banter that inevitably would follow during these visitations. There was a conversation that followed concerning some scriptures that got brought up by Patrick, which he discussed with the two elders, who were accompanied by two younger novices. Patrick had brought up the scriptures that pertained to the spirit of supposed followers of Christ relating to testing the spirits, whether they are of the spirit of Christ or the spirit of the antichrist. The scripture says that any spirit that confesses that Jesus Christ is come in the flesh is of God, and any spirit that does not confess that Jesus is not come in the flesh is not of God but of the spirit of the antichrist. The two elder Jehovah's Witnesses insisted that Jesus is not come in the flesh but was come in the flesh in the past. Patrick insisted that Jesus is come in the flesh and that "when two or more are gathered in my name, there am I in the midst of them," and also quoted the scripture that says, "'I am crucified with Christ'; nevertheless, I live, and the life that I now live, I live by the faith of Christ, the Son of God, who died for our lives and rose again and is in me through being born again by the will of God; therefore, Jesus is come in the flesh! If this wasn't the case, then how did I know what was to come in the future, such as the five national disasters that I told you about earlier, which occurred in California in February 1992 through to the end of February 1994, and how could I promise my friend Raul Carnadas in Jesus's name that he would see and experience the storm of February 1992?

Because these people were not filled with the Holy Ghost as promised by Jesus to his disciples before his ascension, they were cut to the heart and their parting retort was to call Patrick a false prophet. They had no scriptural knowledge to support their arguments because their beliefs were acquired from an adulterated Jehovah's Witnesses Bible, modernized and compromised into the English language by their unlearned predecessors and customized to suit their personal beliefs and therefore not the truth—and in Patrick's judgement, diabolically constructed to suit their pride and ego and to be a religion of control.

October 2007: Indiana Wants Me

In the home of Pat and June, Annie, June's identical twin, and her daughter move into their home because of marital abuse resulting in violence. Three years later, Patrick is being observed on an airplane sitting with his niece, Stephanie. Patrick is saying to Steph that she is now going to see a different Uncle Pat.

Stephanie says, "What do you mean, Uncle Pat?"

He then told her, "The Bible says that a prophet is not without honor, except in his own home, with his own family and in his own town. And we are no longer there, sweetheart."

Patrick and Stephanie are now arriving at the airport in Louisville, Kentucky. He and his niece, Stephanie, are now in Linda's car, Patrick's sister, traveling to New Washington, in the south of Indiana. The news on the radio is reporting on the possibility of tornadoes in southern Kentucky.

Steph says that she has never seen a tornado; Linda says, "Don't worry, sweetheart, there hasn't been a tornado here for nine years."

Patrick says to Stephanie, "You will see a tornado, although you won't be able to see that it's a tornado because you will be too close to it to enable you to distinguish the entirety of this tornado, sweetheart. This isn't going to happen for a couple of weeks yet, but it will happen."

About a week later, Patrick is now seen talking to Stephanie and two of Genevieve's friends, David Griggs and Julian Ponce. He is telling them that he has asked the Lord to send a storm consisting of three tornadoes, one coming from the south, one coming from the north, and the third one coming from the east, perpendicular to the Ohio River, and this is because of the evil that he has seen and because of the police brutality that he has been told about. And this will be a sign from the Almighty that He is unhappy with the hypocrisy manifested by some of the churches in the Bible Belt, their support of inequality, and their persecution and oppression against young people, who were often victims of police brutality, amongst the general population, and their many other shortcomings regarding racism and also because of their lack of compassion exercised in their religion, therefore falling short of the patience of Christ. And also because some of the church's leaders were obviously more interested in the cult of the personality, which would be making their viewpoints dogmatic and therefore diabolical as well by asking the sheep to follow them foremost, therefore separating them from the rest and patience of the Lord. This does not apply to all of the churches but to a modicum of their so-called religious churches.

Patrick, Stephanie, and Genevieve are sitting in a house in Charlestown with a bunch of Genevieve's friends, not too far from the local high school, as a storm warning interrupts a radio program announcing tornado warnings, saying that three tornadoes are approaching the area from three different locations. Patrick is very concerned about the animals at his sister's house, so he and the girls get into the car and head over to Linda's house. Linda's house is on eight acres of land. Patrick gets out of the car and heads straight to Linda's dogs and embraces the five of them one by one and communicates with them by placing his head to their heads with his arms around each of the five dogs one at a time, and then with the horse while visualizing an umbrella of grace that he has asked the Lord to place over the property, which resulted in having them all calmed and no longer afraid. He then entered the house with the two girls who were becoming extremely fearful. Genevieve was pleading to go back to Charlestown about eleven miles away, to see if her boyfriend was safe and alright.

The three of them got into the car and turned out of the long driveway and onto the New Bethlehem Road leading to New Washington. After driving about a hundred and fifty to two hundred yards, the car was heading straight into a wall of water with debris spinning clockwise furiously; at this point, Patrick stopped, quickly reversed the car, and drove back to the house.

Patrick said, "Wow, that was the edge of the tornado, girls; there is no driving through that." Thus fulfilling the prophecy that Patrick had said to Steph in Linda's car on the way to New Washington.

The three of them went back into the house. Stephanie and Genevieve were extremely fearful upon hearing another emergency broadcast as they got back into the house, warning that tornadoes were in the area. The two asked Patrick to pray for their safety; Patrick said that he had already asked the Lord to create an umbrella of grace to protect them from the storm. The girls became even more fearful as the sound of the storm came closer and, with tears, asked their uncle to hold their hands and to pray for them.

Patrick held their hands and prayed out loud, saying, "Create in me a clean heart, oh Lord, and renew a right spirit within me, and let the words of my mouth and the meditations of my heart be acceptable in thy sight, oh Lord, my strength and my redeemer. Oh Lord, God in heaven, can you keep us all safe and create an umbrella of grace over all of us and let these two survive unharmed that they may live and become my helpers as well as witnesses of your grace, in Jesus's name, amen." Both of them said amen.

After praying, the girls wanted to retreat to the safest place in the house. They went into a walk-in closet as Patrick followed them and told them to come outside with him so they could understand the extent of grace that the Lord has bestowed upon them, that they should witness this event. The three of them went outside towards the middle of the property, in between the house and the horse's stable and paddock.

Patrick told them to look upward and behold the lightning and said, "None shall touch the ground near us, and you will both be safe with me." The lightning flashes were so numerous that they couldn't even begin to estimate how many there were, although none of the bolts had touched ground near them. The wind could be heard with an extremely loud howling, yet not a hair could be seen moving from neither Stephanie's nor Genevieve's head, both of them having long hair. When everything had calmed down, in the morning, the only damage that could be observed was about a dozen or so large trees which had been uprooted on the south side of the property below the horses' paddock. And the only other damage was to the American and the Confederate flags on the flagpole at the front of the driveway; both these flags were torn into ribbons, like they had been cut with a big pair of scissors! When Patrick saw these flags, he thought, *How appropriate and righteous are your judgments, Lord.*

Linda's Hot Hands and Hannah's Healing

Malcom is now observing Patrick, still in Indiana, sitting with his sister and his niece, whom he brought with him from England; the three of them are sitting on the veranda at his sister's house. Patrick is telling Linda about the time that he and his son, Chris, along with Amanda and her baby daughter, Hannah, were driving back to Arizona from Linda's house because their brother DJ had called Patrick and said that their dad had another mini stroke. Pat had been driving for quite some time while Amanda slept after her stint at driving. It was in the middle of the night when Pat fell asleep at the wheel and started to drift off the highway.

Thankfully, Chris woke up just then and shouted to his dad, "Wake up, Pappy; you are going off the road."

Pat awoke and quickly regained his composure, and they left the highway at the next exit, which was very close by. They proceeded to drive to a rest area that had a gas station and a large shop attached to it. They went in and got a couple cups of coffee to drink.

While they were drinking the coffee, a woman who was with her brother in a parked vehicle next to their car had approached them and said, "Hi, do you guys believe in Jesus?"

They replied, "Yes, we do; why do you ask?"

She said, "The Lord told me that I can help you. What is the problem that's laying heavy on your heart?"

Pat told her about his father's condition, i.e. the high blockage in his main arteries and in his heart valves and how he was having multiple ministrokes quite frequently.

She said, "Oh, that's why the Lord has sent me to you, as that same condition had affected me, and I nearly died and had a bypass and artery transplant and still came close to death, when some really nice people that were Baptists laid their hands on me and prepared a homeopathic remedy consisting of apple cider vinegar, garlic, and honey, and I took the remedy and then had a miraculous healing following the consumption of the remedy that they had made for me, and I'm sure that it will help your father as well."

So, we told the old man about this chance meeting, and their father, Lawrence, said that he would like to try the remedy, but he would first like to ask his doctor if it was safe to take. So, they laid hands on him and prayed that the Lord would heal him by the power of the Holy Spirit in Jesus's name. And then Patrick had prayed over the homeopathic remedy that he had prepared after speaking to his dad's doctor, who had advised them that the remedy would not be harmful nor would it be of any benefit, as Lawrence needed two major operations, and he wasn't strong enough to survive one, let alone two. Patrick asked the doctor if his dad would last until the beginning of November, as it was now the end of August, and he would not be able to return from England until November at the earliest. The doctor replied that his dad would be lucky to see his birthday, which was three weeks away, and also said, "Nothing will save your father now."

Patrick's father took the remedy for six days, and on the morning of the sixth day, Patrick and Chris were awoken by Lawrence, and he asked them if they wanted breakfast; they both replied yes. After breakfast, Patrick had noticed that his dad's vein definition had returned to his arms and that he was warm to the touch. Lawrence stated that he was going to take Butch, his dog, for a walk; Butch was a Great Dane-Rottweiler half-breed, a very large dog and somewhat unruly at times; therefore Pat thought, *Wow, this looks like another one of God's miracles!*

At this point, Linda said, "My hands are extremely hot, some people have said that I have healing hands."

Patrick said, "Place them on Stephanie's forearms."

Linda did this, and Stephanie jumped with the surprise at how hot her hands had been. Linda then told Patrick that her eight-year-old granddaughter Hannah had been diagnosed with cancer and that she had a tumor the size of a tennis ball inside her.

Patrick said, "This must be one of the reasons why the Lord has brought me here, we should lay hands on her and ask the Lord to heal her in Jesus's name." Linda agreed.

Hannah was due to be taken to hospital in Chicago for an operation. On the morning that she was due to leave, before she left, we got together, and the four of us, Linda, Stephanie, Hannah's sister Giovanna, and Patrick laid their hands on Hannah. Linda asked the Lord to destroy the tumor and to burn it with the fire of the Holy Spirit and to put it in the trash in Jesus's name; we all said amen. The doctors opened Hannah's body and were surprised to find the tumor burnt like it had been incinerated and had moved from her bladder and into her gallbladder. The doctor removed the gallbladder and dispersed it into the thrash. The tumor had left no trace of cancer until this day and only a dent was left on the left side of her bladder, being the size of half a tennis ball, where it previously had been lodged. Ten years later, without any knowledge of her miraculous healing, Hannah went to university in Texas and became the valedictorian of the university, studied theology, and desired to become a missionary serving the Lord.

Easter Week 2000: Dad's Prayer and March 14, 2023 in Jerusalem

When Patrick finished telling the pilgrims in the Church of the Holy Sepulchre the story about hearing the voice of the Lord and the lightning prophecy that followed, he continued to witness to them about how he had also heard the voice of the Lord in his dad's prayer.

Patrick had flown from London, England, to Phoenix, Arizona, to pick up his father from the hospital after his father had triple bypass surgery on his heart. Patrick arrived at the hospital in Phoenix in time to pick up his father from the recovery ward and drove to his father's house. This was the Wednesday preceding Easter weekend in the year 2000. They arrived in the evening and got some food at a restaurant and then went back to the house.

The following day was Maundy Thursday and, in the evening, Patrick's father said, "Son, I'm going to go to bed for a while, as my chest is hurting quite a lot at the moment, we will talk again a bit later."

Patrick said, "Okay, Dad, I will just watch the television for a while."

The volume of the television was pretty loud, as his father was a bit hard of hearing. Suddenly, after about fifteen minutes, the volume of the television went completely silent and the screen went blank. Patrick then heard his father's voice from within his dad's bedroom, from within the living room in the house.

He heard his father say, "Please God, don't let me die now, not while Pat is here, let me die when he goes back to England. Please don't let me die while he's here, he's too soft, he would just fall to pieces, he's got such a soft heart."

Patrick then heard another voice that replied to his father's prayer with, "Don't worry about him, his faith can move mountains."

His father said in a questioning voice, "His faith can move mountains?"

The other voice repeated, "His faith can move mountains."

"Within a few moments?" Then Patrick's father repeated his prayer, asking God not to take his life while his softhearted son was present.

The voice of the Lord retorted, "Don't worry about him, his faith can move mountains."

Lawrence then said yet again in a questioning voice, "His faith can move mountains."

The voice of the Lord repeated, "His faith can move mountains."

It then became quiet, and Patrick said to himself, "What is the meaning of this, oh Lord?" He then looked through his father's Bible and after reading quite a few scriptures, said, "Okay, Lord, it's not for me to question your will but to accept your will, my God."

Patrick then went into his dad's bedroom and sat down on his father's bed next to his dad and said to him, "Well, Dad, so you think that you're going to die while I'm here. I heard everything that you said to the Lord about how soft that you think that I am and how you asked the Lord not to take you while I am here, because you think that I wouldn't be able to handle your death and how that you think that that would tear me apart. I also heard the Lord's voice telling you not to worry about me because, as He said to you, that my faith can move mountains and how you questioned the Almighty saying, 'his faith can move mountains?' And the voice returned saying, 'his faith can move mountains!' And then when you repeated the prayer again and the Lord again told you not to worry about me and He also repeated to you that you should not worry about me because the Lord had told you that 'his faith can move mountains' and yet again, as if astonished, you said, 'his faith can move mountains?' And the Lord repeated that 'his faith can move mountains.'"

Lawrence then said to his son, "How do you know all of these things, as I wasn't praying out loud but in my heart, and in my mind, son?"

Patrick then said, "Well, Pop, the good Lord opened my hearing in a spiritual and celestial way. I believe that it's part of the blessing and anointing that God has given unto me by His grace and through the name of His Son Jesus Christ. Pop, I heard all this as if I was sitting on the bedside right next to you."

Lawrence then said, "Has this happened before?"

Patrick replied, "Well, no, not exactly, but I have had similar experiences, not like this, Dad, this was a first for me. Anyway, Dad, you're not going to die for quite a while yet, but do you remember that man in England that I told you about, the managing director Paul Trapmore? My boss at St. Ives, Peterborough, the bloke that accused me of trying to take the company for a ride when I extended my stay here with you last August for five-and-a-half weeks. Well, they accused me of trying to manipulate the wages clerk to get the Bank Holiday pay after you collapsed into my arms when you had another mini stroke. And then when I rang them up and delayed my return for a second time and then they accused me in front of the pressroom manager, this dude called Michael Clayton, who just happened to be one of my mates that I worked with for eight years on the same crew most of that time, and he told me all about their perceived judgment of my motives for extending my stay in Arizona, which was partying and having a good time. So when I got back to work, I wrote a letter of grievance because of these comments discussed with Annette Remmert in front of my mate, Micky Clayton, which was an insult to my witness in the Lord, and I had also left a footnote with the scripture that said, 'After the first or second admonishment, deliver such as these unto Satan for the destruction of the flesh that the spirit may be saved in the day of our Lord Jesus.'

"So before the end of my last shift, I had explained the importance of the situation at hand to Laurie Thacker, my number one pressman, and asked Laurie if he could stay at the factory until Mr. Trapmore had arrived for work and warn him of these things. Laurie replied, saying that he was too tired to wait another three hours before Paul would arrive at the factory. So before I left work on Monday morning, I went to go and see Gary Fuller the FOC and explain to him that he had invoked the scripture referring to reprobates and how they must be delivered unto Satan for the destruction of the flesh that the spirit may be saved in the day of our Lord and asked him to go and approach Mr. Trapmore for me, to warn him that he must get the apology to my house no later than Maundy Thursday. And on hearing this, Gary totally freaked out and declined the request. Then he looked for Kevin Harding, the deputy FOC, to explain that he had invoked those scriptures and what it meant, that if not, Mr. Trapmore would die, according to the scriptures, on Good Friday. He couldn't find Kevin, so because he was still very concerned, he also told the two committee members, one being Carlton, one of the reel store-men, the same message and asked him to warn Mr. Trapmore that these things were going to happen to him, because once the scriptures had been invoked there is no turning back. And the final man of these additional two blokes was Tony Dinatale, an Italian chap that he had hoped would pass on the message. Anyway, Dad, that man is way too proud to apologize to me, and because of this, he will die tomorrow on Good Friday. Although, Father, you will stay alive for some time yet, so don't worry about it anymore, Pop. You can rest assured that I am telling you the truth."

Patrick got back to England a couple of weeks later, and on returning to work, someone approached him and asked if he had heard the news. Patrick said "No, what's the story then?"

The work colleague said, "Paul Trapmore died on Good Friday of a heart attack."

Patrick said, "Oh Lord, so nobody warned him."

And shortly thereafter, Tony approached Patrick and looked him in the eye and said, "I have no doubt that you are responsible for the death of Paul Trapmore."

Patrick replied, "Did you warn him as I had asked you and the three other dudes that were asked to warn him?"

Tony replied, "No, I didn't warn him as you had asked."

Patrick said, "Neither had the other three."

Impossible Storm as Foretold to DJ O'Malley

Malcom now observed Patrick speaking with his father; he was telling his dad about the evil that he had observed while in the Phoenix area and Maricopa County and that he had asked the Lord to send a storm to flood the entire area.

Patrick's father replied, "How can you do that, you know that your brother and I live here in Glendale, the center of the county, at the bottom of the valley. You're going to have to ask the Lord not to send the storm or your brother and I will be victims of the flooding."

Patrick replied, "I cannot ask the Lord not to send the storm as I have already asked Him to send it in faith."

His dad said, "Well you are just going to ask Him not to send the storm."

Patrick said, "It's too late, as I have already asked Him to do this in Jesus's name."

Patrick's dad retorted, "What about your brother and me? We both live in the middle of the county; do you want us to be flooded?"

Patrick said, "Look, Dad, I will ask the Lord to keep Glendale dry and free from flooding."

Patrick's dad said, "That's impossible; Glendale is at the bottom of the valley."

Patrick said, "With the Lord all things are possible, and don't worry, your feet won't get wet, I promise you in Jesus's name, Dad, that your feet will not get wet at all, so don't worry, you will see this happen, and you will be astonished and so will many others because this will happen for the glory of God."

Patrick returned to his brother's waiting car, and he and his brother, his son Chris, and his brother's wife Gloria drove towards the airport, stopping at a car rental company on the way so that Patrick could have a conversation with the owner about the charges for the broken windshield that his brother had punched one evening on the way back from a night out. The owner said that it would cost one hundred dollars to replace because it was a flat screen, although the curved one would cost four hundred dollars to replace, but then charged Patrick's dad four hundred dollars. The owner, Mr. Sabana, answered Patrick's enquiry by pulling a pistol out and saying, "You can get the hell out of here."

Patrick returned to his brother's car and told his family what happened, then Patrick went back outside of the car and took off his shoes and shook the dust off them and said, "Vengeance is mine, says the Lord, and I will bring judgment upon this place in Jesus's name."

The family then drove to the airport. Upon going through security, Patrick said to a policeman that he should investigate Mr. Sabana, the car hire dealer; the policeman replied, "Oh he's a good man; he supports little league baseball and other good causes."

Patrick said, "Would a good man pull a gun on someone making an enquiry into certain charges being disputed having made no threat whatsoever?"

Patrick then went to the gate with his son to fly back to England and home. Patrick got a phone call from DJ and Gloria; Gloria was saying in an excited fashion how the FBI had investigated Sabana and had him arrested on various charges, and he wasn't the man that he pretended to be.

After a few days, Patrick watched the news on television; an unusual phenomenon had happened in the USA. In Maricopa County, Arizona, a typhoon or monsoon had hit the county, flooding the entire area with the exception of Glendale, which remained unaffected and completely dry and untouched by the flooding, this being the lowest point in the entire county, seemingly impossible although visibly and undeniably so, as the viewers of the news program had observed and witnessed on camera, while the lady reporter had stated that the impossible has happened, as the deluge from the storm had not flowed into Glendale, the lowest point in the county!

Patrick phoned his dad a couple of days later and said to his pa, "Well, Pappy, did you get your feet wet?"

His dad replied, "The strangest thing happened, the whole Maricopa Valley flooded except for Glendale, right at the bottom of the valley."

Patrick said, "Have you forgotten that I said to you that I would ask the Lord to keep Glendale and your feet dry when you bitched at me about me asking the Lord to send the flooding while at the front of your house the day that I left for Sky Harbor?"

Patrick's dad said, "Oh, you're right; I must be getting old."

"That's okay, Pappy, everybody that gets old tends to forget things; it's not a big deal."

November 1973

Malcom is now observing Patrick meeting his in-laws for the first time, having a meal at the dining room table with June's brother also at the table. They finished the meal and retired to the living room and sat down to have a conversation. Previously, June's father had asked Patrick what his intentions were with his daughter; Patrick replied that he wanted to become legally married to her, as they had a wedding ceremony in London with the Children of God group.

Patrick and June got legally married at Gateshead Registrar, which was then on March the 28, 1974, with June's mother and sister in attendance as witnesses. Patrick had his immigration status sorted out and became a bona fide resident of the United Kingdom through marriage. Patrick and June had a child and named him Christopher. Patrick lifted his son up into the air above him and said, "I dedicate this child unto you, my Lord, and if it is at all possible, bless him with double the faith and spirit that you have blessed me with in Jesus's name, oh Holy One."

Back to America: May 1975 to December 1976

Malcom observed Patrick as a young man back in his native roots in the San Fernando Valley after first spending a week at his sister's house when she still lived in California, after arriving from England with June and his son Christopher. Patrick started working as a roofer with Hans Ritt, a friend of his dad. Hans was a remnant of WWII who served with the Luftwaffe and had won the Iron Cross. Hans was of questionable character, having manifested anti-Semitism in front of Patrick to an extreme measure. After a couple of weeks, Patrick had an argument with Hans and subsequently quit working for him.

Patrick then started working for his uncle Cappy at the then-modern equipped truck and auto repair garage, able to accommodate eleven vehicles at a time. Patrick worked for his uncle for about five months and had found out that his uncle had been defrauding him through his wages by reducing the labour cost on Patrick's copy of the labour by twenty percent, whereby paying his nephew fifty percent of eighty percent of the reduced labour cost to the customers. Patrick then confronted his uncle about this deception and ultimately quit working for his uncle Cappy and never worked for him again.

Patrick then started working with his good friend Rick Ward, who was the foreman at a printshop that specialized in printing computer forms as well as insurance and various business cheques. Patrick worked there for nearly a year when his wife June had been informed that her grandmother was dying. And in the interim, there arose a problematic issue with June's immigration visa application. Patrick got in touch with the immigration office and was informed that if June left the country, they would have to start the process all over again in Edinburgh. June went back to the northeast of England at the end of July that year, and Patrick followed her there in December of the same year.

Previously, while still in Van Nuys, Patrick worked as much overtime and saved as much money as he could. Patrick's sister and her second husband, Lee, had moved into the bungalow and shared the rent, enabling Patrick to save enough for a deposit for a house purchase back in the northeast of England. Patrick then acquired a one-way flight to London and left California in mid-December 1976.

Before Patrick left for England, his boss, a Mr. Ed Doty, told Patrick that he would give him a very good reference and stated that he would hire him again anytime; in fact, he would give him a job, even if it was just for a couple of months, and he would give a pay raise of a dollar an hour, and "If you want to go back to England and then come back again for another period of time, I will give you another dollar-an-hour raise, and if you want to come back a third time, I will give you another dollar-an-hour raise. And I will also hire you any time, even if there's not any vacancies. I will give you a job and also give you another dollar-an-hour raise, that's how much I think of you, and I will say as much in the reference that I am going to write for you, Patrick."

Patrick flew back to California three times over the next twelve months, working for two-and-a-half months at a time and then flying back to England to be with his family. Ed Doty kept his word and rehired Patrick and gave him a dollar-an-hour raise each time he returned from England.

Camping At the Kern River: Late Spring 1976

After having lived in an apartment building for about three months on Sepulveda Blvd in Van Nuys, just up the block from his brother's house on the same side of the street, Patrick and June moved into the two-bedroom bungalow next to his brother's house in a cul-de-sac situated on Sepulveda Blvd with some old friends, Roy and Marsha in their bungalow right across the driveway of DJ's house with another school friend, Rick Ward, and his wife, Sheila, next door to Roy's house. The four couples had agreed to go camping for the weekend, with the Kern River being the destination. They traveled in three vehicles, one of them being a pickup truck with a camper on the bed of the truck. They arrived early evening and made a bonfire and had a mini party until bedtime. Everybody got into their sleeping bags and retired for the night. In the morning, Patrick got some firewood to boil some water for tea and coffee. He then went to the river to fetch some water; as he approached the river, he observed a young boy aged between eight and ten struggling to get out of a swirling current next to a large boulder on the far side of the river just a few feet from the rapids. Patrick kicked off his shoes and ran towards the river and dove in, swimming towards the child, and upon reaching him, he got a hold of him and pushed off the rock to get the momentum that he needed to get himself and the boy out of the current and swam safely with the boy and approached the shore. Roy saw what was happening, helped Patrick, and brought the boy the last thirty yards out of the river, and Roy returned the child to his parents, who were unaware of the situation and that their child had nearly drowned.

Late 1977: A New Year; a New Job in England

After, Patrick started working with his good friend Rick Ward. And Patrick's wife, June, had been informed that her grandmother was dying and about the problematic issue with June's immigration visa application. June went back to the northeast of England in July that year, and Patrick followed her there in December of the same year.

After three trips back and forth to California, on the strength of the reference that he had received from Ed Doty, Patrick applied for a job with Soag Machinery based in Brentford, Essex. The managing director was so impressed with the reference he got from Ed Doty that he hired him on the spot right away. And he started working for them in the new year. Patrick and his wife had saved enough money to put a deposit on a house in Tanfield Lea in County Durham in the northeast of England. Upon returning to the UK, after the third return trip to Van Nuys in one year, when he had gotten the job on the strength of the reference that Ed Doty had provided, he started working as a print demonstrator/installation engineer and traveled all over the United Kingdom for the next three years. And he stopped returning to work in America at Accuforms in the Valley. And with him travelling about fifty thousand miles a year for Soag Machinery, his new employers, and with him being away from home overnight quite often, his wife, June, became angry and fed up with Patrick's absence from the family home and asked Patrick to quit his job, as his employers had also wanted him to work in London for an extended period of time as well. Patrick handed his notice in and became unemployed on the first of May 1981.

Spring 1977: Exorcising Demons

During one of these return work trips, Patrick had been telling Bill Heath, who was Gloria's cousin, about the Lord and how to receive salvation on several occasions, until one day when Bill arrived back from a Northern California vacation and had proclaimed to Patrick about his conversion and rebirth into the faith. Then Bill had proposed that he and Patrick should go over to his Aunt Grace's house and tell her the good news. Patrick and Bill are now at Grace's house. And while at Grace's house, Bill started to explain to Grace about his conversion to the Christian faith through the process of being born again. Furthermore, Bill asked Grace if she would like to become a born-again Christian as well, to where she replied, "Yes." So, Grace got onto her knees, and Bill asked her to repeat after him, and Bill said that she should ask Jesus to come into her heart and to grant her salvation. At this point, Grace found it extremely difficult to repeat the prayer and unexpectedly became overpowered by a demonic spirit that manifested its voice through Grace Palmero's mouth. The manifestation carried on for some time and became very difficult and forceful. Bill was astonished and afraid by what was happening. At that moment, Patrick prepared to exorcise the demon, which became even more difficult and verbal, stating that they were not interested in Grace but rather more interested in Patrick. At this point, Patrick pled the blood of Jesus Christ over Grace's body and ordered the demons to depart. The demon left her body, and Grace received salvation readily and thankfully and had no memory of the previous possession.

Summer 2012: A Cancer Scare But Is There Humor There

Patrick is seeing Dr. Farrell, and after getting a prostrate examination, the doctor tells him that he has a swollen prostate gland and should get a biopsy to investigate the condition. Patrick has had his examination at the NHS Queen Elizabeth Hospital in Gateshead and is in the changing room in his dressing gown with four other men, also in their dressing gowns, waiting to see the consultant to get their results after having an MRI scan to determine whether the cancer has spread. Patrick has his meeting first while the other four patients wait in the changing room. The consultant tells him that he has Gleason 7 on one side of his prostrate, Gleason 9 on the other side, and a PSA reading of 11.2, which translates into a diagnosis of terminal cancer. The consultant says that you will have to take measures to deal effectively with the problem, or you will die.

Patrick walks back towards the changing room, and in his mind, he starts to sing, *I've got cancer, prostate cancer, I've got cancer, prostate cancer, who could ask for anything more?* And then as he opens the door to the changing room, he continues to sing: "I've got cancer, prostate cancer, I've got cancer prostate cancer, who could ask for anything more, who could ask for anything more," and imagining the other four patients joining in, singing and dancing in their dressing gowns, with each one of them having a shiny black walking stick and the five of them continue singing: "We've got cancer, prostate cancer, we've got cancer, prostate cancer, who could ask for anything more, who could ask for anything more?" And still imagining as a pretty nurse walks past the five of them still singing with gusto and dancing: "We've got cancer, prostate cancer, we've got cancer, prostate cancer, free Viagra, free Viagra, who could ask for anything more, who could ask for anything more!" By the time he gets back to his car, he is laughing his head off and says within himself, "Wow that was so funny; I thought that I could even hear Jesus laughing as well."

When he got home and told his wife about the diagnosis, she started to cry. Patrick told her not to worry about him. And then he relayed how he had received the diagnosis with his imaginary song and dance routine and sang the song for her, which made her laugh her head off as well, and she said to her husband, "You are so crazy; I never know what to expect from you, Pat! I love you so much."

And he replied while hugging her, "I love you too, darling, don't worry. I still have a lot to do before the good Lord is ready to take me back, so I'm afraid that you're going bear with me for a while yet."

Summer 2022

Patrick is talking to Ron and telling him how he had written lyrics for the first time when he had met Brian Yerberry in Tenerife while on holiday in October 1986, the last time that Halley's Comet could be seen in the earth's skies. Brian had written some rock music and asked Patrick if he would want to listen to it. Patrick listened to the track several times and told Brian that he thought that it was pretty cool. Brian then said that he was trying to write some lyrics to go with the tune but could only come up with "breaking the chains" and asked Patrick if he could think of some lyrics relating to "breaking the chains"? And that is when Patrick first got emerged in lyrical endeavors. And a while later, Patrick wrote, "The Face of the Woman." And he is also telling his good friend Ron Johnston about the evening that he met Kenny Lee Lewis, a former member of the Steve Miller Band during the production of the *Arc of a Diver* and *Abracadabra* albums and was meeting him at his home in Woodland Hills, California, after making an arrangement to purchase one of his guitars, a beautiful 1955 Gibson L4 archtop, single-sharp cutaway in sunburst with f-holes.

Patrick rang the doorbell, and Kenny answered the door and invited Patrick into his home. As Patrick followed him, Kenny's three-year-old daughter ran over to Patrick and hugged his right leg while the pet dog ran towards Patrick and jumped up onto his left leg. Kenny exclaimed, "Wow you must be alright; the dog and my daughter both love you; come on in and meet my wife as well, have a seat and I'll get you a cupper."

Patrick, Kenny, and his wife then had a conversation about Christianity, and Patrick informed them that he had written some lyrics that were written in the spiritual ethos of the Christian outlook.

Kenny said, "Have you got them with you?"

Patrick replied, "Yes, I've got a set of copies in the car."

Kenny said, "Go get them, and we'll have a look."

Patrick got them out of the car and returned to the dining room to discuss his lyrics with the couple. Kenny said that he really liked what he had read so far and asked if he could keep the set of copies.

Patrick replied, "Yes, of course, I have plenty more copies in the house." Then Patrick explained how the band Guns n' Roses had made an offer of twenty thousand dollars to buy the rights for his lyrics. And although after talking to a copyright lawyer that his sister worked with, he was advised to retain a minimum of 1 percent, which would give him the right to publish the lyrics in a compilation he was working on. Guns and Roses upped the offer by another five grand but insisted on purchasing one hundred percent of the copyright, which Patrick refused. Kenny and Patrick got together in Hollywood at Kenny's gig a few days later. After the show was over, Kenny was saying that he and his wife really liked his lyrics, especially the one entitled "The Woman in The Wilderness"!

PART THREE

Featuring Modern Times

THE BATTLE

Reeling from the battle
Feeling lost in the legend
On my way back from the war
Clothed in a garment
I had not seen before
Wounded though just now
I cannot feel the pain
The spirit of love came
Love eased the pain
It healed the wounds of the soul
And victory emerged in the battle
That brought the miracle of the war
It was evident there was no sign of any scar
Now my mind is clear and my vision is upright

THE WOMAN IN THE WILDERNESS

When a woman comes of age, I'll still cherish the child in your heart
When we were young, it was such a different outlook and love came so easy
So easy that it helped us to solve the question that kept us from letting go
Our hearts leapt at the suggestion of love
It put us on our feet to the music of the song
We never thought of stopping
Not as long as we could dance and move to the rhythm of the song
Until our souls became one in the spirit of the song
When a girl becomes a woman will she listen to the sage
He's picked a hard-chosen moment to rescue from the rage
The waves of fear were lapping all around
The children of her heart were scattered about
Their lifeline was in the words of the song
It can happen in this kingdom of the heart
Change the course of destiny for the spirit in which we have longed
All life yearns for the love that exists in the lyrics of that new song
Caught up in a place where we just want to be
Where we just need to be, where we just know we belong
Love carries the children of her heart on the wings of the song
Woman of the wilderness, the children of your heart have become one
Rescued by the love in the lyrics of that new song
The love in your heart created the calm
The hard-chosen moment released us from the storm

INDIAN SUMMER AND THE FACE OF THE WOMAN (October 21, 1986)

The face of the woman dressed in the shade
With a veil of gossamer her shame has no refrain
She is a sorceress her gift is bound in chains
She preaches the love of money listen to her bay
Baying like an ass, seek monetary gain
As she arrives from her dwelling in the cities haze
With conquering love listen to my name
Conquering soul breaking those chains

When you hear my words, you will know my way
Sift the heart to retain, is what's left classified sane
Confusion, delusion, the illusion remains the same
Strength through weakness let another take the flame
Strength through weakness a paradox in a phrase

Will the sorceress discover what's waiting in the wings?
When the heart recovers lost thoughts of another waiting for the change
Let's sing a new song of deserts bathed in the rain
Indian summer eclipsed by the promise of love, feel the rain
Indian summer eclipsed and no longer bound in chains
Indian summer eclipsed by the sharpness of my blade

With conquering love listen to my name
Conquering soul breaking those chains

WHO CAN STOP THE TIDE? (November 1986)

Some say that calamity's biding time
Were the authorities wrong?
While Armero paid the price
All my brothers cried
Yet how many others tossed a coin
And still they couldn't decide
Now let's be honest
We are here propping up our pride
We are here just to live our selfish lives
Now the tears, they rose as a mighty tide
And now what's this, we hear
Folly strives in an abundance of hard-hearted lives
And the tears, they rose as a mighty tide
Giant quake about to shake the foundations of our lives
Who can stop the tide? Brace yourself for a deluge of what's about to arrive
I'm a Californian brother that can't stop wondering why
It's better to take cover than live to love a lie
Can you stop the tide?
No more tears for misfortune
Spirit's gone for a ride
Ashamed and confounded

The residue will be delivered to a lie
Who can stop this tide? Halley's Comet, yeah
The seventy-seventh time that it's passed by
One seven left before the rising and the tide
Seven days, seven years
Aftermath will take its path
Leaving a flood on the nation's pride
Tears that rose as a mighty tide
A flood of tears journeyed through the years
One was lost but now has risen with the tide
Forty days the number of the riddle
Will the world survive?

YOUR HANDS
(January 8, 1993)

When the diplomats of folly gather for the final spin
The esteemed of nations sow seed from a bag of wind
The future investment is in the spirit of man
It's time to cultivate an airtight rock-solid plan

There is a new order to the world, clap your hands to the scam
Sign on the dotted line love that money in your hands

Democracy plays the host, rock and roll stage a show
The Soviets change course and the sandstorm blows
Old Babylon glowed for the mother of its wars
Group of Seven, vote to make their pledge to the Whore

There's a new order to the world, clap your hands to the scam
Sign on the dotted line love that money in your hands

A gathering of wizards crave to be each head
A hundred drums are beating, there's a con being bred
There's a million dollars waiting, for the first to say, "I'm in!"
Just one second gone and all the free phonelines jam
A billion takers are shouting, "What's it going to take
What's it going to take, what's it going to take, to win?"

THE NIGHTMARE THRIVES
(August 11, 1992)

A season of summer invades winter's domain
A flood threatens from its dark icy terrain
An exodus of nomads crowd into the playgrounds
The foraging for delight, spawns an eerie fright
Echo from the mountain bound across man's insight

The darkness chimed, "Who's next in line?"
Morals decline, but the money is all mine
The poster cries, "Wanted dead, not alive"
Looks like the haunted time has arrived

The mourning for ashes will follow soon
The clashing of symbols bellow out doom
The cloak of confusion paves a dark way
Preceding a message placed in the grave
As the grim reaper appoints the final day

Man's hourglass gets trapped in the corridor of lies
Confused minds play host as the nightmare thrives

A reception's being held in the foyer of tied limbs
To celebrate the race being staged on a track of quicksand
As the picture clears, a dark and evil creature appears
And stands ready to strike with the hot iron in its hand
To brand his victims with the desired number of man

The darkness chimed, "Who's next in line?"
Morals decline, but the money's all mine
The poster cries; "Wanted dead, not alive"
Looks like the haunted time has arrived

ARE WE REALLY ALIVE

A blank piece of paper, a hollow vapor
Religion starts a new caper rest assured cries the prayer
Can the ruse sustain the plot of pain?
Will the lie defuse as the angry lose
Who can choose to win or lose?
Can words make this body bleed?
Sword of sorcery strikes an evil deed
Monetary values exceed in a den of thieves
Procrastination of the dark seed
Pluralism in idyllic greed
Truth or lie bears the weight of the find
All comes out when finally scrutinized
And some cry, "Are we really alive?"

Summer 1985

"Then said he unto me, 'Prophesy unto the wind, prophesy, son of man, and say to the wind, "Thus saith the Lord God; Come from the four winds, O breath, and breathe upon these slain, that they may live."' So, I prophesied as he commanded me, and they lived, and stood upon their feet, an exceeding great army. Then said he unto me, 'Son of man, these bones are the whole house of Israel: behold, they say, "Our bones are dried, our hope is lost, we are cut off for our parts." Therefore, prophesy and say unto them, "Thus saith the Lord God; Behold, O my people, I will open your graves, and cause you to come up out of your graves, and bring you into the land of Israel. And ye shall know that I am the Lord, when I have opened your graves, O my people, and brought you up out of your graves, and shall put my spirit in you, and ye shall live, and I shall place you in your own land: then shall ye know that I the Lord have spoken it, and performed it,"' saith the Lord." Ezekiel 37:9-14

THE HEARTBREAK (January 13, 1993)

We weave a solution and choose simple pleasure to jest with our pain
Face to face with your inner self, there is no beginning to what has no end
Then comes this encounter, where thoughts wrestle the wind
Sometimes the heartbreak communicates an end
Sometimes the heartbreak resurrects a friend

When delight chases desire with whispers of shame
And solitude is overcome and dances in flames
We are no longer caught in the crossfire of pain
And are free to find ourselves in a circle of friends

What evolves in a song's love is waiting at the gate
A wise man said, caution casts shade along the way
Another man crossed a barrier where fire dances on the wind
And returned with power to revive all of his friends
Sometimes the heartbreak communicates an end
Sometimes the heartbreak resurrects a friend

A KEY IN SEASON

We've all heard it said, to everything there is a season
And a time for every reason to be realized
And there's an event that occurs to everyone
Life's goals are never lost when we strive for love regardless of the cost
Imagination couldn't duplicate the cost that's been paid
The key to the heart is reaching for the last of the lost
A signal in the night, A beacon of love illuminates the hearts of mankind
Singing the song of joy in the face of adversity
Shell-shock circumstances torture the romances of simplicity
When the key to the heart touches the familiar cord
You'll know what the morrow brings
Distance doesn't exist in love's philosophy
No circumstance could distract from the romances of love's simplicity
We will always be lovers with hearts touching in a perfect day
I will give my love to you in full bloom
Our love will grow from the romance of simply holding on
Holding on to love's strong infinite song
The key of love is like the warmth of the son
I will just thank the Lord for the gift of love
Love's for all that accept the fact that love is for all
The only toll on this road of love is your soul
It's hard for the soul to reach for mercy as it needs a clear vision
Let the vision of the soul be enhanced by love's light

The death is the doubt and doubts may cloud the skies
But the truth of love will clear our minds
When one can pass beyond one's doubt death is gone
And the key to the heart is the love that survives
Feast in the fact that our love can stand against the tide
And day breaks and shakes the soul free from the lie
Knowing in spirit that love stands astride our lives
The time for love is now the time
The winds of change come and the Illusion appears
The prison is a prison of fear born of doubt
Then love appears and the desert of sin is but a grain of sand
A once-sea of sand swept away by the gift of love
The song of the dance of shadows disappears from one's sight
In the heart of the olive branch the oil is life
In my heart is the key in season Freedom from the existence of strife
Conflict has gave way to unity time has gave way to life
For the key of heaven harken to this heartfelt cry
Soul searched solution came as a beacon in the night
A key in season slipped through bypassing the lies of modern times

THE PRESENT AS IS AND ALWAYS

The time is ripe for defiance. This is the time for rebellion, for people that depend on truth and righteousness to deliver them from the confines of dogmatic judgment. There is not a more critical time than now to rebel against the trust that man has placed in uncertain materialistic riches. It is time to defy and to fight against the power of the beast. Let me ask you this: Can the pursuit of a temporal advantage develop into a foundation whereupon man could belay his trust and build thereon to establish a solid refuge where shelter could be found in times of trouble? The trust in uncertain riches deprive the development of spiritual growth, thus breaking down the defenses of one's own faith until a breach is established, giving place to doubt, thereby exposing one's vision to a kaleidoscope of confusion and disillusion.

BRAINSTORM TRAGEDY (1986)

One more brainstorm tragedy
And this man says that he's going to capitalize
Monetary gains in the government's lies
Brutalize the poor and force them to eat humble pie
Feed the people a purposeful pact of lies
Brainstorm tragedy with media magic
To plot a course from an uncharted source
Will the victim be the poor?
And who will help him through the door
Will the road be paved with gold?
It's just another tragedy with the bottom out of the floor
When the sickle strikes and the threshing has begun
Will the manipulator stand his ground?
Without a sound of sorrow and a heart of stone
On unhearing ears will the plea fall as if to gall
I've come to capitalize on government crimes
Media magic to plot a course so tragic
Condemning the young innocent's vision
To a kaleidoscope of confusion and abusive lines of type
Will the piper arrive in time, will the piper arrive online
And blow the lid off this
Another brainstorm tragedy
Perpetrating government crimes

May 13, 1987

The Lord said unto me, "Write down my words that you may give them to my children, that my people may know my will and obtain my guidance. The seeds of ambition were instigated by the deception of Eve at the beginning of time in the prompting of disobedience by the father of lies. The seed of ambition can bring about but one ultimate fruit, a separation from the love of God, which thereby deprives oneself from being in the will of God."

The seeds of ambition give birth to envy and jealousy, causing one to covet after another's achievements, that a person may obtain an item of desire, such as a possession that they believe would bring them deliverance from their own wantonness and the desire to present themselves acceptable to society in the accomplishment of achieving their goals, yet they find that they have not attained contentment. In the light of this, people turn again to whatever new thing that the manufacturers have developed to entice the people of the world, to lust after an inanimate object. This in turn would cause them to consume folly unto their souls by creating a graven image for them to bow down to and worship.

There are some that will disregard this simple deception, for they seek a far greater evil: to lust for power, that they may exercise authority over the people under their rule. Either direction they resort to pursue the desire of their heart can only bring about the downfall of their own soul and an enlightened quality of the spiritual life. Because of a lack of motivation purely founded in the love of God and a genuine concern for the welfare of our fellow man. The knowledge of the truth has become harder to grasp. Because of this, the fruit of ambition has caused the earth to be covered by the deeds of darkness that are prominent in our society of today.

This being brought about by the birth of capitalistic ideals. These ideals have instituted stagnation in the growth of the spiritual life as outlined by the Word of God. We find, "Delight thyself in the Lord and He will give you the desires of your heart," as in the words of David. Likewise, in the words of Jesus, we hear, "Lay not up for yourselves on earth but lay up for yourselves in heaven, for where your treasure is, there will your heart be also."

This world that we live in today has laid many traps to ensnare the souls of mankind. The ace in the hole is the love of money and the power an abundance of money can bring to the possessor thereof. Money is in itself not evil, but rather the evil is in the abuse of the stewardship of how this medium of exchange is used, and the hoarding of it is where fault is found. If the love of money is the root of all evil, then what is a government that prides itself on ever increasing the abundant wealth of its capitalistic supporters through financial coups, such as war dressed up in their democratic garments, causing an influx of tribute into the coffers of their spiritual fathers, the lords of destruction, furthermore deriving profits from the natural resources of the earth for the benefit of the few?

The motivation behind privatization is to help aid the ensnaring of the masses by giving them a taste of usury through a limited proportionate share issue to establish the enticement of the deception. Therefore, the poor are lured to come and buy their article of luxury through hire purchase and furthermore issue the people with credit facilities to enable evil to force the people to regard wantonness. People are ensnared because their virtue of responsibility is held in judgment, and humans naturally do not want to appear to be ignorant of their own actions.

By this, spiritual blindness comes to the foreground through the smokescreen of capitalism and into an attitude of monetarism. This is a direct effort by satanic powers to indoctrinate the people into a world of finite boundaries, causing the spiritual life to become dormant and the awareness dimmed, thereby inducing the folly that is in the worship of the graven image.

Can an earthly utopia exist in this so-called civilized society that man has created for himself, with its ignorance of the plight that it has developed for the growth of the inner man, thereby depriving it from the peace that resides in the contentment of the soul, where spiritual awareness is achieved simply by being in the will of God and that through hope and faith? The Lord has said, "How long shall the land mourn, for they have made it desolate, having raped the resources of the earth without temperance and to enable them to establish their idols in the false wisdom of ungodly rule, following the guidance of the darkness in their spiritual wilderness."

"Let the oppressor glory in the work of her hands, the unequal scales of balance, and the abominable fruit of their unholy ambition to exercise rule over my people whereupon she would extract the blood of their spirit." The Lord says, "I will reward her with that thing she fears most. Therefore," thus said the Lord unto me, "a sword, a sword is sharpened and is also furbished, and it will strike in the heart of her lewdness and will destroy the deceit of her indiscretions. And they shall cast their silver into the streets, and their gold shall be removed: their money shall not be able to deliver them in the day of the wrath of the Lord; they shall not be satisfied nor content because their wantonness is the stumbling block of their iniquity, but the poor shall be redeemed, for they have placed love above desire and life before time."

COMPASSION FOR THE COMMON MAN

The failure of the world will perish throughout all the land
No longer deluded by the confusion of pride's game
For this pride will be burnt in the heat of love's flame
Expedient changes captured by a passive aggression
A moral spark ignites the fire of this flame
The eternal fire consuming at its own desire
Mankind's shame and this pride is just another name
The benefit is lost in the cost of playing that game
The creation of love in the heart is not in a simple way
The celebration can commence through the marriage of pure spirit
With exposed distractions consumed by the heat of the flame
The creation of love in the heart is not in vain
Like the participation in a pointless game
Exposing the distractions to be consumed by flames
Amidst gathered conclusions that were born of mankind's shame
Conquering love, spirit of life, and the Word of Light
Advancing against mankind's wayward life
This is one man's desire and Everyman can enter in this way
A hard-chosen moment close to the fear in our common shame
Destruction of the stark terror amazement at what takes place
Compassion for the common man disperses during the disease
Yet still many are crying the tears of blood shed by man's lack of love
These tears will be eclipsed by an onslaught of God's love

This is the remedy that will wipe away any trace of hatred's blade
All can be forgiven and start anew with a clean slate
With words to be easily distinguishable from a position of poverty
Possessions lost to awareness setting the soul free
heartrending emotion and inspiration discovered the food in this cupboard
Treasure hidden in the heart can be freely received
Once again within reach of love's sane breed
Laughter gate crashed my humor looking at myself yet again
I thank God that I'm a failure in mankind's worldwide destructive plan
I'm going to rely on compassion for the common man

ECHO IN THE MOUNTAIN

Through one door and men are on the earth
Through another door and man is in the world
Like the love of a woman there is a life love plan
Torn between the treason of reason burning in the flame of desire
Foraging delights in the heat of the fire
Inner corruption mourns for ashes once again
Sound asleep in slothful consumption fully aroused at the punchline's sham
While madmen find no joy in laughter a coastal collection on a shore of sand
Flatter the confused coalition of an exposed affliction
What is your privatization plan racialistic hatred Bigotry PLC again
Anchor the soul to promote wantonness who are you trying to kid
Might as well stage a race on a track of quicksand running a race with tied limbs
The entry form is a deception and reception in the foyer of the 666 man
The enemies of Christ pervading with a larger darkened light
Shine those trophies of desire some say life is just a game
Place them on the mantle all too near to the flame
They will burn on the hearth of shame weigh the dross in the balance
For the hire of man poor captive in an ungodly economic plan
Echo in the mountain the shadows are wearing thin as a downward swing descends

Credibility is issued with a nomadic passport in your hand
Time has ended for the echoes behold the desolation wind
Holy Ark of the new covenant naked here I stand
Pride-less faith the power to change a man
Quiet in confidence born again though not by the will of man

APRIL 6, 1987

The motivation of true religion is not to establish a structure of a so-called modern nature such as exists in today's traditional churches of traditional dogma. Some of these go through the motions with a preponderance of a holy attitude, thus leaving the larger portion, that of their own souls, to yet hunger for the fulfillment and comfort that is experienced in the peace given by the Holy Spirit of God through faith in Jesus Christ, the true and just Savior of humanity. Christians of America and the world, question yourselves and search for spiritual peace by exposing your own motives for your salvation. How can any start to love their enemies when they find it so very hard to love friends and neighbors? Though there be a large and varied diversification of religions, there is only one church, and that is the spiritual body of the bride of Christ.

In this body we are all joined one to another in the communion of the soul in the endeavor to enter the love of God. The motive of the Holy Ghost is to bring together the souls that make up the body of Christ into the spirit of the bride that she may bring forth through the gathering of our members, one of another thereby delivering the spiritual family of love. The true church of God is built on this foundation of love and that all members of the body be brought into this fold through love and not through dissimulation, but rather in the harmony of spiritual unity conceived by returning to the Lord and His Word. We the members of His body shall say unto him, "Take away all iniquity and receive us graciously; neither shall we say anymore to the work of our hands, these are our gods." Faith is the key that unlocks the door of the truth and exposes the lies of discord that has deceived the children of the inheritance from its guidance of love and into the dissimulation of the various and rightly called hypocritical churchy religions of today. The Lord said unto me, "No more will I abide the faithless daughter that turns to the witchcraft of hypocrisy."

Therefore, stating trust will be put in my treasures of silver as in those that lead me in the demonic guidance of the gods of the television screen, for the purveyance of their message to the masses, "Follow me, for this is the way," while that television preacher asks for money from the poor and spiritually hungry souls of the congregation, while sitting on his own ill-gained fortune. He is therefore establishing the ludicrous of their self-promoted ministries. The Lord will dissolve all these so-called churches of today that the children of God may enter into the oneness of the true church, and that the true believers may have their understanding opened unto the spiritual wisdom and love that exists in the kingdom of God. And the churches out there in the world that say, "We will follow the way that Jesus has paved," these will be rewarded with grace, and the light shall guide them. No more shall the brothers and sisters of love be the victims of the lies and hypocrisy that is experienced in the vain competition of the abominable fruit of sectarianism. The Lord himself shall divide his people, the sheep from the goats, that we may fight the true war against hatred and lies. This shall be achieved by the Holy Spirit of God Almighty and shall be enhanced by the love of His sacrifice, His only begotten Son.

You are either with us or against us. If you are not with us, then you fight against the power of love and the inspiration of the faith found in the Word of God. There is no victory to be found in the rebellion against the law of God's love; what remains is loss in one's own soul in the turning away from the simplicity of the love of God. The unity of the church of the Lord is found in the blood of Jesus Christ and not in the doctrine of modern man's intellect and the interpretation of carnal understanding. The gift of God is the freedom of salvation in the love that exists in the eternal power of the spirit of God. Noah was a man who saw the gift of God's grace through his faith, which is "the substance of things hoped for, the evidence of things not seen."

This is the foundation of the spiritual realm of love's true existence that is found in the Word of God. In these times of spiritual darkness, vision and light shall be given to many. This has already been given to those who were not a people; these shall be called the people of the most High God. God himself has ingrained in them the spirit of meekness and a genuine desire for the truth. The Lord said to me, "This I say to all my people, come to the fountain and drink of the water of life freely, for the wisdom to be found in my love and the spirit of truth shall open your hearts to enable you to digest the bread of the latter growth, until the fullness of time be accomplished. The woman of the wilderness shall be hidden from the evil consummation of the last days of wickedness. The time is upon you, it is even at the door, flee as a bird to your mountain, the Mount Zion of the Israel of God, the existence of the spiritual realm of God's love given to the inheritors of faith. As sons of Abraham by faith and through the blood of Jesus, the Son of God;

the redemption from death will be to him that enters into the dimension of love, where separation from the confines of time shall be born into fruition. Time has come for spiritual stagnation to be overcome by the power of love's concern for the welfare of the soul. The nourishment of the life-force shall grow from the seeds of salvation, to cause the soul of the bride to grow together into an army of truth and righteousness, in one body, by the will of the Lord and by the power of His own hand. The Lord Jehovah does not require the help of any to fulfill His will, for in Him and through Him is all that exists in life, the good and the evil, the love and the hate, the power of the arm, and the power of unlimited knowledge." The Lord said unto me: "I have come to heal the wounds and to open the prison doors of unbelief, that the time of the Gentiles be fulfilled, as spoken of by my holy prophets. This is the revelation revealed that I have caused my witness to write unto you, the truth of my will. I have called him, for in his weakness, my love has made him whole."

BAPTISM
(Early December 1987)

It was conceived in conclusion
Love to conquer all fear
No problem hasn't a solution
No price is too dear
The creed of compassion
We must swallow this seed
An instant cohesion
And we are freed in our need
What of man's declaration
Contemplation in temptation
To fulfill lust and greed
As hatred rises compassion recedes
Crash of '87 prophesied
Yet did any take heed
While the next step
Israel baits the Arab League
The Jew's taste for blood
Will it recede?
And this, a time of great need
The beast has risen
Shall desolation be a desired trend?
Wall Street will crumble again

The whore's foundation stripped by her friends
Religions falter as seed sown to the wind
And houses built on a foundation of sand
There is a solution
Let your soul be born again
Cultural differences dissipate in love's flame
The depths of our longing mold into one
Compassion reaches beyond and on
As the chains of condemnation meet their resolve
Fruit of victory in the defeat of self-esteem
Celestial connection can be achieved
When most graciously received
Regenerate in the baptism of the flame
This is spiritual war, not a flesh and blood game
Hatred is our enemy, falsehood is the ally of shame
With God's love, we will never be ashamed

AN OLIVE BRANCH
(Summer 1986)

Are you ready for a new branch for humanity?
Injection of the word, the kindred of love
Lose the sour taste, when you finally let go
The oil of the olive branch flows
Set in motion, nothing stops destiny
We can hear the sound of commotion
Let's hear the harmony
Arriving of the wind of unity
The depths of the ocean in my heart compel me
I'll tell you sister, tell you brother
You're only going to get love from me
Yeah, you're only going to get love from me
When I was a boy
I searched for the soul of love constantly
When I became a man
Complacency tried to strangle me
The debris of capitalism
Too many victims
The debris of fascism
Too many victims
The writing on the wall states the truth to all
Can you see the depths of the ocean in my heart compel me

Is this the last week; Seven days, seven years?
We're going to see who really cares
Must be time to walk away from complacency
When everything is left in the past
And the first shall be last
Then only love will shine
Create a clean heart in me
I've said before and I'll say forevermore
You are only going to get love from me
Love is not a chore that had to be worked for
A broken heart opened the door to love for more
The case for joyous laughter never dies
When love opens the eyes to a future without lies
And injustice has to die
You are only going to get love from me
Like oil from the olive branch flowing free.

THE WARRIOR
(December 30,1986)

He gathered the armaments prepared for the fight
The strength of his arm was in the spirit of his might
The words in his mouth created a flame in the night
The reward of his deeds were not the motives he held in sight
He came to free the captives who were imprisoned by lies
Exposing the distractions that held them in the night
The night's darkness brought about by materialistic values
The abundance of inventions in which we waste time
Lost in conventions created for these last times
The warrior stood in the gap while the children regrouped for the final flight
He and his brother were given the power by the hand of the king
Sent for the purpose in completing the ring
Alpha and Omega one in the same
The heart of the warrior was fashioned in the flame
The flame of the truth is the strength that overcame
The warrior in himself was nothing all the same
A mere man who was opened in his hearing by the voice of the king
His heart was broken and his spirit was contrite
He feared when he heard and when he read the words of God's light
He trembled and bowed at the thought of his sight
Some trust in horses some trust in lies

Your cars are the chariots of the last days in which you hide
With an abundance of idolatries the distractions preceding the flames
Warrior in the world, lift up the staff, give honor to His name
This new thing I do, summer in winter, light in the shade
Snow in the desert on Christmas Day
The power in my Word is the sharpness of my blade
Able to create something in which no man can lay claim
Man marketing God's assets for unlawful gain
To promote oppression the continued pursuit of shame
Now I have wounded the enemy, the beast is that shame.

JUST BEFORE MIDNIGHT: MAY 30, 1987

The Lord has shown unto me a great evil and men who have become the instruments of great wickedness. The evil that He has shown unto me is the heart of the city. He said to me, "These are the men that devise mischief and give wicked counsel in this city. They say, 'It is not near, let us build fortunes, for what can endanger our prosperity?' These are they that kindle the fire under the cauldron, that stoke the coals of depravity in the theft of the freedom of a man's soul, that say, 'The Lord has forsaken the earth,' and that the Lord does not see, that say, 'Let us therefore continue in our endeavors to cast darkness over the vision of enlightenment, that the people return not unto the Lord in their hearts, but let us further enhance the deception and snare them in our Babylon. This city is our heaven and the birthplace of the merchandise of wantonness, where the graven image is forged.' The abomination is the ploughing of perverseness and the sowing of deception by the lies of their motto: 'Cast your hand with us in gold; build your house with greed, and deliver your soul into hell!'" Therefore, the Spirit of God came upon me and said, "Thus says the Lord, 'With violence I will destroy Babylon, and I will send a destroying wind into the midst of her deception, and all her fortresses shall be spoiled. Babylon is the reigning cities of the world in which is generated the spirit of whoredom, where their most unholy temple of worship is their beloved stock exchange, and the synagogue of usury is where their moneylenders worship. He is a merchant; the balances of deceit are in his hand; he loves to oppress. Therefore, turn now my people, to thy God, sow to yourselves in righteousness, reap in mercy. Break up your fallow ground, for it is time to seek the Lord until He comes and rains righteousness on you; keep mercy and judgement and wait on the Lord, in your patience, your heart will be restored.'"

TALK
(January 1992)

Woke up and got to work down at the prison cells
Feels like I've been swimming in an old dark well
What's seen in the future governments try to sell
Will the ancients return to impose heaven or hell

Talk of the prophets, talk of the sages
Talk of the seers, talk of the major players
Preachers teach you've got to pay with your prayers
Oh there's a lot of talk so what's the next flavor

A desert evades the shade as seconds fade in the past
Enduring a thirst for a future that's born with a mask
The climate screams, utopia's just another lost dream
As the whip grows weary and fears of losing its sting

A vision stirs hysteria to cheer each manifestation
When art is at its pinnacle, fresh from inspiration
Talk of the prophets, talk of the major players
Preachers teach that you have to pay with your prayers

VOICE OF THE HEALING WORD

Voice of the healing Word is about to sing
Can the spirit carry magic in its wings
Soon we shall see a change in our very lives
Drifting on the vapor of love
Waiting for the moment of love to arrive
And being told by a certain friend of mine
The choice of love is deep inside the time is right
The voice of the healing words cry for a sea of lives
Seasons change but love remains to enhance the broken life
Sow the seeds of love for the field is ripe
The voice of love regains the hand of God in the sea of our lives
Children can sing threatening the darkness of the night
As the voice of the healing Word retains the light
Would you agree that the time is right
Is the voice singing out or is just a forty-five
With so much confusion can we discern the face of the sky
The spirit carries magic that has never failed
To heal the tragic broken lives and the broken hearts survive
Voice of the healing love dispelled the lies
Broken hearts are bathed in light the answers to life are in sight
And love eternally abides in this light

WILL SHE RISE, WILL SHE CRY

With so much turmoil and so much confusion
Is it right to call on love for a solution
With so many walls and fences to climb
Is there time to waste on lies
Call on love buy the right
Buy it now without a price
So many think the time is nigh
With so many miracles hidden in the light
Will she rise, will she cry
Sing this song one more time
Will she sing like a sparrow in the sky
So many times that I have tried to ask why
Can you give us love not some cheap line
Can you show us how to resist the crime
Is it a crime to wonder why
And will I know that love is mine
Will she sing that love song one more night
So many miracles are hidden by lies
I have got to know, does love still abide
And will that love overcome the lies
The crimes that have been committed
Through all of our lives
The crime of a soul leaning on a lie

And will salvation yet be mine
Just for the money you know it happens all the time
There's no more time for coaxing
For man to accept the fruit that is ripe
Time's running out, we need to eat the bread of life
When one is uncertain all that is left is vicious strife
We really need to communicate the spirit of light
Take some time for devotion
Freedom in the spirit it happens all the time
And the man has been chosen
From the beginning of the night
It's a heartbroken moment
When that beast receives earthly life
Full of strife and commotion
Are we the prisoners of his might
Just for the money and it seems to happen all the time
Now I'm ready for the fight
Even though nothing could stand in this lonely night
I know that there's a way to obtain the might
And that is to absorb God's Holy light
For this love could always bring more
Than is needed to even the score
Love reversed the damage inflicted upon the heart
An eternal healing by God's steadfast spark
Love has already lit the fire in our hearts
And I know that I am ready for this fight

Though nothing could stand against the dark night
The power of the Word has overcome all
Before the darkness has even come to light
And we are definitely prepared to take the fight

JOURNEY ON THE HIGHWAY
(Late 1986)

As I looked into the mirror, I saw failures turn into fossils of lies
The division of doubt sowed discord and created transgression in life
The clearing of the eyes often takes us by surprise
So many questions and I don't know the answers or the reason why
Then one day it was heard that there had to be a time
A time to face oneself reflecting their own life on the line
I don't ever want to feel the need to have a separated identity
I'd rather sing the song of love in the face of every adversity
Being on the edge and so close, all too near to the abyss
And what's more too often is that I just can't stop wondering why
Can love fill the breach when what's missing is a sound reasoning
Journeyed on the highway and every exit was an aspiration of mine
Quite often these achievements were somewhat filled with strife
Seldom was the night filled with the substance of a loving life
Accomplishments being so unenlightened born in this dimension of time
They were just an example of how great can be the fall of pride
The world rejoiced in revelling—as the question was posed
Can the spirit shine in this journey out of the dimension of time
Was it a lie when it was said that man shouldn't compromise
Indecision out of place sitting on the fence is starting to ache
Sometimes it feels like a love at first sight is just a crying shame
If and when will it happen if your paths fail to cross and meet again
The Truth will find the soul of love yearning for a new beginning

The state of love does not need conflict to maintain sanity
As the words of truth often cut the deepest stripe
The power of healing is in the light of your eyes as the gift of love arrives
This power will cause our souls to reach for the source of this life
The exits on this highway, the systems of convention
The conspiracies of destruction, the illusionary perceptions
These exits will be exposed for what they have always been
Another pack of lies, crass concept trying to force time
With romance tortured and shamed and violated by the love of money
A systematic change and will fortune ever remain the same
While far too many suffer plagues of the brain
Like a wave's might, love will break onto the shore of our lives
Loving forgiveness is the source that kindles and ignites this course
Now is the time for love to illuminate in this night of ungodly forces
The truth will bring it down on its knees
Love that seemed so unattainable is given for free
The way has been opened by the light of love that shines bright
Our darkness has been destroyed by the builder of light
That enlightened the corridors in the highway of eternal sight
The day has been bound unending by the vision of the fountain of life
Tears have been removed by the hand of affection and by its light
Extending from the arm of love reaching into the midst of the night
Set a sentry in your heart for a better life looking for a new day delivery of love
It's not the clothes that makes a man what he's supposed to be
But heart in the soul of his life energy

The gift of love will lay its hand on all that feel the need
They that yield will be given a new heart born of love eternally
The cost has already been paid by blood on the wings of the dove
Questions of doubt completely disappear in the light of this love
No longer being an obstruction to a vision of faith in our spiritual need
Fear gets lost from our understanding, trapped in the corridors of time
People born of God's love are absolutely free
It only takes a small incision to heal the heart of the free
Souls have become one in the marriage of love's eternal prize
The knowledge of love gave birth to wisdom enhancing the light
God in His wisdom has opened the eyes of the blind
Children of one father the redemption draws nigh
With love in our hearts, we will survive
The day breaks and awakens our lives to a vision without strife
With love in our hearts, the truth is clear in our sight
The words that I speak, they are of the spirit and they are life
The door to the way of holiness is in the hands of love's undying life
The path is at the feet of him that came from above
He that was pierced hands and feet by the haters of love
Nothing can stop us from obtaining the gift of God's love
It's free to all ordained before the foundation of time
Losers in society and wayfarers, you are associates of mine
Make ready for the journey, the end of this world's in sight
It's the last days and we are strangers that strive for a better life
What this world has to offer is just too wrapped up in lies
The world we seek has got foundations in the truth of eternal life
Choose to make your destiny free, cast your lot with love and see

LIFE CONTINUITY

When you are looking for love and a life continuity
Unleashed from the bonds of humanity
Stepping free on the promise of sincerity
Street-wise like the children of reality
Sing of lives striving for equality
When one survives these bonds of humanity
The soul alights for a life that real love will bring
If there are clouds in your sky the vision of the heart will see
The righteous are seen to cry there's no more wondering why
Crystal-clear is the love that is brightest tonight
No hardships survive when the final stage comes to light
Unleashing God's Love to brighten the skies
As the truth opens our eyes love will repel the lies
There's no more waiting for the time to arrive
Love will fill the breaches while we're stepping free
On this promise of sincerity as the gift of love
Soared like a glove onto the hand of humanity
Say what it was that opened this door of reality
Mysterious love that welded our hearts in unity
Warriors conquered by the love that this spirit brings
Patient lovers unlocked from their bonds in humanity
Grown of love this power reaches through eternity
Where you can spend all of your life in this love of spirituality

A LETTER CONSTRUCTED ON MARCH 17, 1988, ADDRESSED TO PRESIDENT RONALD REAGAN AND PRIME MINISTER MARGARET THATCHER; COPIES SENT MARCH 18, 1988 TO REUTERS, NEWS INTERNATIONAL AND DESMOND TUTU via the Dean of Durham Cathedral. Copyright March 18, 1988

Hear this word that the Lord has spoken against you, for unto you, the rulers of the United States and of Great Britain is this word sent and unto the whole house of your kingdom and its families. This is the word that was sent unto me: thus says the Lord, "An adversary shall there be, and he shall be round about the whole land, and he shall spoil your palaces and undermine the power of your political empires; strength also shall depart from the hand of him that yields three resources: gold, oil, and the souls of men. Neither shall money nor shall any power deliver you in that day, for I shall say the word and none shall stop its course," says the Lord. Behold the oppressed in Central America, behold the greatly oppressed in South Africa; you have imposed sanctions upon the poor in Panama for the sins of a few, thereby inflicting stripes upon the innocent as well as the guilty. You have not imposed sanctions upon the evil regime in South Africa for the sins of many, while the poor are trampled upon day after day. Therefore, thus says the Lord, "As you have treasured the riches of the earth more than the riches of the kingdom of God, and in this, that you have highly esteemed the love of money more than the love of God, therefore thus says the Lord: I will withhold from you the great rain and the little rain. For now, I *will champion* the cause of my poor and oppressed children, and I shall remove the scepter from out of your hand, and it shall be given to another. I have called unto you, and you have refused to hear; I have called for equality, and you have answered with a false balance; you have taken from the coffers of prosperity and have heaped unto yourselves the lion's share. Therefore, the Lord shall discover the foundation of your transgression and visit upon you the fierceness of his mighty sword, and He shall strip you of your skirts of deceit, and so shall your nakedness be shown unto the nations, that they may fear the living God and have respect for His word and for His Holy One. Repent now, and execute the judgement of truth in your lands, and restore the equity of righteousness, and the Lord will repent of the evil that He has called against your lands. These evils have I called upon you: drought upon the great plains of America and upon her harvest of wheat, and in Britain, I shall bring flooding upon your great city of merchandise, and I shall cause the sea to rise up against your southeastern coast, for the time of the echo is past and the destruction that awaits is near to come. Thus says the Lord: If ye will not hearken to me, to walk in my law, to hearken to the words of my servants the prophets, whom I have sent unto you, then I will make your house like Shiloh, and I will make this city a curse to all the nations of the earth."

SIMPLE FAITH
(Summer 1986)

I'm running to finish the race, but will vanity capture first place
Can the outcome be best for you or perhaps fortune for two
When the wind carries the rain in the sky
Is it an illusion of power, or the soul of our lives
In a dimension of love in my eyes
A vapor of love carried by the tears in my heart
How could man never strive for a just, honest life
A simple faith in love would suffice
A simple faith could restart our lives

Is it pride that stops us from discerning the lies
The lies that have become the stock of modern crime
The regime of nations courting for time
Turning the screw on the fullness of this pilgrim's life
I'm tired of reactive machinations of power supported by lies
Deliver your fear, will it stand by the cry of the righteous
That died for your lives

A simple faith in love will suffice
A simple faith could restart our lives
Will you stand with this pilgrim,
Or let vanity capture first place

Dread and destruction
In exchange for bread on a plate
Short-changed by this system of hate
Is love just a pipe dream
Or, has there been some mistake
Come on someone
Can you tell me the result of the race

THE ROCK AND THE ALONE

When I was a younger man life would never leave me alone
The song on the radio the sound of reaching for more
She's never letting go she's found a place called home
Freedom of truth never failed she's always shone
Let's open our ears to the cries of the alone
And bring home bread of life young man stay here for a time
Everyone sees that the time is running out
The songs on the radio the sound of reaching for the heart
Here is one for the alone there's time left for brotherhood
Even if it has to come from the stones
The rock the stone and the alone of the earth
Will reach and be quenched from thirst
Bread of life will be first revived from the dearth
Love of lies vanished in the thirst
The song on the radio the sound of reaching the goal
Nothing could be on the wire slowing life's truth anymore
The time has come to seek the good of love's store
Bread of life restores the heart once more
And then the song on the radio expels all distraction
And love plays its song once more singing set your heart for eternal life
Love never dies the song on the radio cries love never dies
The song on my radio the rock and the alone and yet not alone
As we all come closer to the dawn

BORNE TO THE BURDEN

When the burden falls
What seems to be hard and heavy—And the light only illuminates
What already seems open to our eyes
Take away the veil and reveal that we need to make us come alive
We were born for a reason
We're climbing the heights we were born for a reason
Children of the burden piercing the night
Hold on to each other hold on through the fight
We were born to the burden and our souls seek to soar
For the light yet again the question's asked
As we cry for the right who will guide us
As we fight off the lonely night
We see the veil is lifting
Corruption is dead and gone with the night
And the oppressor has left this earthly life
Prisons are opening being bathed in light
Man is born again full-grown
Complete in one and passed through the night
Hold on to each other
Not for yours but for their precious life
For the children which were borne of the burden
Have escaped with each other
And have pierced the night
And the light illuminates our hearts
In the vision that got the victory over the night

CONDITIONED IN THE FLAME

The message is now complete
The seal of love has left wickedness in defeat
Soldier of love relished in the flame
Delivered his soul for the mercy to be found in the Savior's name
Blaze of love to conquer man's hate
Soldier of love commissioned to open the seal
The bittersweet taste of the last chapter in the book of love
A respecter of persons he was not beguiled
Listener of song singing holy love's claims
Time brought a man by the hand of love
To deliver the children from the grip of hatred and war
An increase of faith by the hand of the Lord
The daily sacrifice is about to be restored
Now is the time of the last watch let your hearts be filled with the oil of love
Lifting your hearts from the depths of the flames
Caught in the trap love laid its claim
Arise in the miracle shown in His name
Netting your hearts and souls to be cooled by the love that is the goal
Time to let go and let your heart speak for your soul
Man of the world is conditioned to lies and to pride born of fear and shame
Man of the soul is free to soar in the heat of the flames

He cannot be hurt the seal is set the heart is given a new name
Love opened the closed door to the future and love burst through the flames
Now the children can grow in the love of the soul
Freedom cannot die, freedom doesn't know time
In the dimension of love the time of the prophesy's vision is alive
Gog and Magog it is close to the end of time
Light your lamps with the oil that won't run out by the hand of the Lord
Jesus is his name, resistance can only bring about shame
Open your heart and pronounce His name
Love will feel lifted and bloom in the flame

MARCH 16, 1987

This message is directed to all on the behalf of the voice of commandment, given by the Holy Spirit of God. I am neither a religious scholar nor a member of any denominational church of society; I am a man that has been opened in his hearing by the voice of the King. The Spirit of God says, "Publish the truth, give bread to the poor, and warning to the wicked." This is the word that I have received from the hand of the Lord: "If a man divorces his wife, and she goes to live with another, shall he return to her again? Shall not that situation be as folly derived from circumstances born of lust rather than that of love? Can a bridesmaid forget to enhance the beauty of the bride, or can the bride forget to don her wedding dress? Yet the people have forgotten the Lord days without number. The people who call themselves the saved of the Lord, without meekness, and the people who say, 'We are lords; we will come no more to be reproved of God, for our work and our play is the fruit that we shall eat of our own labour.'

"The abundance of their distractions in which the people hide from hearing the Word of the Lord will be as though it never was, and the secret hiding place shall exist for none, but your nakedness will be discovered because the hard-hearted have refused to be ashamed. Yet these people say, 'I am innocent, surely His anger will turn away from me,' and those say, 'I blame God, look at all the evil in the world, the destruction of the poor and the killing of the innocent.' This is man's own doing, the fruit of lust in the establishment of idolatry, the pleasures of the flesh, and in the easing of the burden by trusting in the appliances and the chariots: those highly esteemed cars in which lay store the invention of your own image brought to life by your trust in lies. Again, you question in your hearts, saying, 'How can God be a god, when did He bring us any good thing, was it not our own two hands that provided all these goodly things, the item of which we spiritually place in our beds, that we have knowledge of them as of a sexual partner?' Turn now, my people, and let your heart be stripped of the delusion that lies to your mind, and I will heal you," says the Lord. Will He reserve His anger forever? Will the people not cry unto the Lord, "Teach us to put our trust in God and in the Holy Spirit of truth and place our faith in the name of your Christ"? For the scripture says: "For out of the north shall an evil break forth unto all the inhabitants of the land, for the lack of love towards the Lord thy God and towards your neighbor, the deceit of unlawful gain for the vain pursuit of your delicacies. Prepare the way of the Lord in the secret places of your heart, for He will come with healing in His wings." For this is that day of which it was said, "Let no man deceive you by any means: for that day shall not come, except there came a falling away first, and that man of sin be revealed, the son of perdition, who opposes and exalts himself above all that is called God, or that is worshipped; so that he as God sits in the temple of God, showing himself that he is God," the god of forces which man has turned to, to worship the abundance of his devices. Babylon the great, the mother of harlots, is that spiritual wickedness that is the foundation of the motives behind free enterprise, the instrument used to fuel the greed that man uses to justify himself of the lust thereof and to make himself a god that is no god. God, the father of all, is a jealous God; he will have no other god before Him. Man has turned his back on God, yet He has extended his hand to an unwilling recipient of His love. Men and women of the earth, you rulers of the realm, you build your bulwarks up to the height of the heavens that you may protect your possessions; know you not that a man's life does not consist of the things which he possesses, but a broken heart has the Lord prepared, and out of this heart will proceed the power of love, to heal the wounds, to open the eyes of the blind, to cause the deaf to hear and to bring understanding to the heart of the hungry. That the children that be born of God's love may enter into the rest of the Lord and into the spiritual Israel of the living God. The Lord Jesus is now at hand; "For I live," says the Lord, "And all shall hear my voice." The voice of God thunders, and who shall stop the hearing thereof, though Satan himself be manifested and deceive many, yet shall the will of God be performed, and none shall stop it. I have fulfilled many prophecies in your eyesight, yet you perceive them not. All eyes shall see, and all ears shall hear of the man that will be called the "Statesman of Statesmen," and say, "Him shall we follow, for who can resist his power and his wisdom, which is the deception of sin, the denying of the validity of the Word of God, and the pertinence of God's Word in today's society." The lie will be fulfilled in the need to create a peace that is no peace, and that will be bought with your souls in exchange for the misconception of knowledge. How many tragedies must man witness to open his sight to the folly that lies in the trusting of many inventions? Can these protect man in the unseen future that lies before all the people of the nations? The fate of the Herald of Free Enterprise and what caused the severe shock of this disaster, was it not the reward that must have been delivered into the hands of the oppressor, the manipulators of capitalistic endeavors, belaying their trust in the graven images brought to life in the fullness of time and in the transportation of sorrow by the methods in which man has abandoned his mind, body, and soul from acknowledging the fear of the Lord? The man of this world and its society have chosen to grieve the Holy Spirit of God, thereby making of no effect the sacrifice paid by the blood of Jesus Christ for our own inability to control our hearts from being deceived by the lies that speak to our minds after that truth has first spoken to our hearts. This name, the Herald of Free Enterprise, that was cast symbolically in the dawning of a golden age, bringing hope of riches to fulfil the lusting of greed for the diet of evil men, prepared the way for the denial of love and brotherhood as lived by the early disciples of Christ, where no man called anything his own, but they had all things in common, in order to enable them to deny oneself greed for an uneven balance to create "profit," that magical word that drives mankind to self-destruction, where economies collapse unless peace is held at bay. It is high time for all that will side with the Lord God to adopt into their hearts the spirit of God's love and to fight the true war against the counterfeit conception of true Christianity that exists in the realm of the spirit and in the hearts of the children of God. Have faith in the Word, for the Word was made flesh and did dwell among us and does still dwell among us in the love of God. The righteous are taken from us before the evil that is to come and none lay it to heart, so has been the demise of the innocent lost to tragedy after tragedy. The beginning of sorrows is upon the kingdoms of this world, and the time has come for all to mourn; will the merchants mourn the loss of lives to the calamities or their covetous profits gained by deceit, sustained by the oppression of the poor and righteous people of God? The merchants of free enterprise and the merchants of usury shall have their reward. As foretold by the mouth of Jesus, "In those days, there shall be wars and rumors of wars," your new cold war, "and there shall be earthquakes and famines and pestilence shall fall upon the nations of this world." The media cries out a warning, "Fear AIDS, for it can kill you," yet many do not perceive that the AIDS virus is a manifestation of a pestilence that shall kill and cause many to fear the power of the plague. The virus is a disease; a pestilence is a judgment from God; the plague of the pestilence exists in the transmission of the evil curse because the motive behind the sexual act lacks the foundation of the communion of love that exists in the realm of man's soul. The transmission of this curse is evident in the abuse of the body, which is the temple of God, for God dwells not in temples made with hands, but a body has the Lord prepared. As prophecy foretold, "A wicked and adulterous generation seeks after a sign." The sign that has been given has not been seen because of the lack of faith to acknowledge the realm of the spirit as seen by inner vision. Safe sex does not constitute the real love between man and his neighbor as sanctioned in the kingdom of love. God has control of love because God is love. The illusion of love that is really lust exists in the spread of AIDS through a counterfeit act of love. Man must first put his heart right with God before he can experience real love and act in the faith that simplifies the justification of life's existence in love, as ordained by the greater love than that, which is known in the so-called freedom of the mind with the mind's blindness of love; the comprehension of love comes through the heart and not with the understanding of the mind. If man is to fight to free himself from the threat of these curses, he must first become open to the vision of the terrain in which this war of love and evil rages. Detach your souls from the prison of your mind, and love will possess you always.

THE EYES OF THE BLIND

The choice of freedom is hidden in the heart
The loss of reality can infect one's judgment with a hard heart
Man has tried to cross a Savior with an upstart
False prophets false religions loose change from the wrong source
Who can correct God's truth nobody wants lies and hypocrisy anymore
Standing on an island situated in the north
The children of the world can they endure
Can they carry on without taking notice of the writing on the wall
They wrestle for advantage in the contest that's set before
So many profess to see their darkness is their woe
Open the eyes of the blind cause the just to receive their reward
The choice of freedom is knocking on the door
Inner vision is available and nothing can stop it from being restored
Turning your back on the gift of love just doesn't hold store
This realization brings joy hereafter
It exists in spite of what man thinks is the score
Can any convince me of a lie in which I could place store
Can a building house a free spirit that has been freed from the world
Alive and in this body Love gives its reward
What man needs is regeneration of the soul
A clear conscience that doesn't have to be worked for
Strength made perfect in weakness how could it have been worked for

When the choice of freedom that's hidden in the heart
Is forever found it's an abundant overflow
Standing on an island situated in the north
There are many children of the world and many will be children of the truth

THE BATTLEGROUND

The battleground is set in the field of misfortune
The greater loss is sold for the pride in confusion
The concentration of the mind is in the quest of ambition
The loss within the fight is the lack of conviction
The ground your feet attains disguises your sight from inner vision
When alone and in the territory of self-promoted rendition
Let your heart carry the sword
Remove it from the hand of diverting devices
When truth is known folly lies exposed
We can't hide from the nakedness of our secret vices
Inventions of delusion conclude the indiscretion
And the heart is filled with devious enticements
This battleground lies within a realm of spiritual retention
A kingdom separate from this world of physical dimensions
Love exists in true conclusions that offer the heart rejoicing
The pity is man's lack of faith to recognize this
The mind offers its varied resources
And through the heart the mouth speaks
Mankind asks, what more could there be to life
The view is limited by what the heart will allow to be scrutinized
All too often man is inclined to accept situations compromised by an alibi
This action only helps to justify acceptance of lies in the fear of our mind

If this were not the case, there's one thing you'd have to face
Could man afford to pay the price?
To deny the mind the luxury of being self-righteous
War rages in the field of pride versus pride
It will not take long before the cost is the loss of love
This battle can be won it need not be lost
Victory will come when the heart surrenders
And the love that takes over wields its sword
A lasting foundation will be restored truth will open any door

THE CHILDREN'S NEED

The children run, they skip and play
Oh for man to have such a hideaway
Laughter flows from their lips at whim
The innocence of children can create mercy for man
For their fears they find comfort within
Give an ear to my proposed plan;
Let's look to the children, learn from them
It doesn't take much to forgive a friend
The sound of their singing is a whistling wind
The loss of their joy would cripple us within
When you hear the sound of silence
Will we sink or will we swim?
The days are coming for the foundation of sand
Who can hide from the storm within?
A father gives to his child concern with his hand
A hand for one another in this volatile system of man
Love's lack of affection stifles the growth within
Hold on to the awareness of love's lifelong friend
Children, they grow, they learn to cheat and to slay
Perpetrators of war, stealing your love away
Economies collapse unless peace is held at bay
What kind of solution can come from the creeps of today?
Fascism, capitalism, communism, they all harbor destruction within

What kind of establishment can call themselves our friends?
When they all esteem wisdom to be kindred to sin
Trust in your peers when their motives are plain
Theft of your faith, they'd you place it in them
Man's got a history, can greed and folly stand
And who needs to be told, let not man turn your hope
Into a religion of sand, a fanatic's justification to slay his fellow man;
Our redemption can only be bought by the blood of one man
Children they rise and they glow and find love once again
In spite of the coaxing to grow up and become a man
If there's a plan for destruction, there must be an alternate plan for man
I'll look to the children and find hope once again
I'll look to the children and find kindness steeped in love from within
I'll look to the children, God save them from the inhumanities of man

THE ESCAPE ROUTE
(Summer 1986)

My venture from out of here, although it was in the past, it is still very clear
I had wrought from within an acquaintance I now call friend
Through one door and men are on the earth
Through another door and man is in the world
Like the love in a woman, there is a life-love plan
Torn between the treason of reason, burning in the flame of desire
Forging delights in the heat of the fire, inner corruption mourned for ashes once again
Sound asleep in slothful consumption, fully aroused at the punchline's sham
A coastal collection on a shore of sand, while madmen find no joy in laughter
Flatter the confused coalition of an exposed affliction
Racialistic hatred, Bigotry PLC again, what is your privatization plan?
Anchor the soul to promote wantonness who are you trying to kid?
When the princes of peace gathered before the final din
Earth groaned in the spirit, what proceeds the madness of man
Greed in a credit card numbering the sadness of man
A selection of a cumbersome collection of sin going through the motions
Summit of nations disaster within a false sense of security
Souls sold for external possessions, ground gained for the wind

Another reception being held in the foyer of the 666 man
Weigh the dross in the balance of the hire of the man
Captive in an ungodly economic plan
Echo in the mountain, the shadows are wearing thin, as a downward swing descends
Credibility issued with a nomad's passport in your hand
Time has ended for the echoes, behold the desolation wind!
Holy Ark of the new covenant, naked here I stand
Prideless faith, quiet in confidence, the power to change a man
A terrestrial solution can never win
Crucified with Christ, born again, God-given gift of love, repent and win
The power of love will reign in spite of man
You hear it on the airwaves, you see it on the screen
Why's this world racing to the Apocalypse?
It came from the future, it came from the past,
It is still very clear in spite of the deceptions of man
I had wrought from within, an acquaintance I now call friend
Escape route ventured on the wings of the wind
Vision restored in the clear spirit of my friend

WILL JERUSALEM EVER BE THE SAME?

Was it meditation or a spiritual medication that brought me to this game,
Was it just a plan of foolish laughter that disguised the pain?
Jerusalem will it ever be the same, some say a city of the future
Oh yeah, a city with a past, when the holy breath cried in a tender birth,
The spirit soared, heaven touched the earth, all the failures of the world
Vanished in the dirt.
Some say the plan of foolish laughter will save you from the dearth
Where can we hide to be happy when we live on Planet Earth.
A celestial takeover could never fail or do worse.
The wayfaring men, though we be fools, could not err therein,
And the ransomed soul shall obtain the everlasting goal
Jerusalem will harbor the truth once again
It is written in the stars, it is written in the earth,
Can a wrong ever nullify the truth
Was it meditation or a spiritual awakening that brought me here once
again
Some say the foolish laughter, though we live on Planet Earth
Oh can you tell me, will Jerusalem ever be the same?
Will the children laugh, will the mighty roar, will the table be set amidst
the time of woe?

DEMOLITION OF THE HEART

No well I just say no
There's not going to be a compromise
It's got to be a demolition of the heart
Before we can start to survive

Yeah and some people are saying
We've got to change this man
Before he starts to realize
After a demolition of the heart
It is us that he may well surprise
Oh yeah and some people may say
We've got to put him in his place
Before he's set to fight us with too much space

They are all trying to bring him down
But what they do not know
Is that when he comes around
Their own judgment is going to turn them down

Enemies and foes tried to compromise us
Oh yeah but they were too late to demoralize us
Because a demolition of the heart
Gave us the head start

Even before they started to fight us
There's not going be any compromises
Because our values have already been galvanized

It's going to be a demolition of our hearts
That justifies us
Yeah it's going to be a demolition of the heart
That cries for the righteous

THE PRODIGAL'S SOLUTION

My love of life is a perpetual motion
Like the waves of the ocean
Being tossed about by this sea of emotion
I once had a notion in love for you and me
I was seeking a solution the problem was
I couldn't see no I couldn't see
I was forever putting myself before you and me
I hope we come to learn the answer
To create a love of life reunion
It will take a lot of honesty
To rid ourselves of all doubt
And bring our dreams to reality
Life the perpetual motion
These waves in our ocean
Is how many venues that there will be
Before our final devotion
In this vast sea of emotions
Yes I once had a notion
For love in you and me
Willing our dreams to become reality
It looks like no more time for doubt we see
The only time left is for harmony
Stronger than the waves of this ocean

Is this prodigal's loving reunion
Is this the prodigal's only solution
I hope it is will you see
We'll have our love for eternity
This is the prodigal's only solution

LOVE WILL BE THE BOND

When hope for tomorrow started to crumble and fade, I found myself trying to run away. The weapon was lowered for the aim, the target remained the same, I was looking elsewhere in which to place the blame. Standing on the laurels of a lousy lie, a vision held shaded by self-satisfaction. My forward moves kept losing traction, I tried to keep myself happy and did not even ask why. When my understanding opened, it was only myself that was being framed, by dogmatic notions that limited the gain and time lost to different potions, the truth in freedom has never changed, a change of costume only enhances the shame. The truth is, an agreement has already been signed, as the time is ripe for love's eternal prize. It is ready to break onto the shore of our lives. Love will be the bond that welds our hearts into one and hope for tomorrow will never die. The poor of the world can't afford to live a lie, where the cost of self-satisfaction seems far too high, especially when it is achieved through a delusion of grandeur, an exercise in futility that can't open our eyes. Heartfelt words heard in heartfelt cries, they will find the hope in love and the reason why, love will expose the distractions and the lies. The truth will be yours; the truth will be mine, all who hear my cry, return to love beyond the realm of time.

STOP THE GENOCIDE

When a man's mind and the heart collide, an incident turns to accident in a young man's life. And when the need arises to take a strong hand in the saving of a young child's life, the newspapers cry with the tears of youth's sore eyes. Let's stop the genocide! The innocent's life is dear, there is no measure to the price. Too much perversion in this time of life. Got to curb this gender, putting the yoke on the young child's life. If any hear my words, take a stand throughout your life. It's time to stop the genocide. When the heart and the mind collide, we've got to catch hold of the spark of life. Let the fire burn in the brightness of your eyes. It's time for a change of the propaganda that's publicized. Television's gospel is looking like a pact of lies; rebellion is looming in the night. A system of false solutions casting a veil over the lies you've only got yourself to vacate from the prison of man's lies. Diplomats of folly trying to steal the fullness of life. Consecrated to the delusion that it's not cool to be upright. It was created in the heart, love to dispel throughout all time. Left in a prison of cruel torture, we've got to stop the genocide, the innocent life is dear, there is no known measure to the price and the vision becomes clearer as we grow closer to the dawn. When the heart is worn and torn apart and the world is given back to its deeds, some will say, fall to this passion, it may fill the need. Lord help us to sow the seed, love is the same in every creed. When the heart is nourished and love's claim is staked to the tree, it's not just an inheritance of our ancestry. Love is the magic that fills our needs. Oh, love is not some kind of commodity; love is real, a lifelong necessity. Mankind is confronted by love, and it seems like only a few know that it's free.

The choice of love or folly and the heart is nourished or worn and brought down to its knees. When we have left for the future, wisdom cries in the streets when the poor are gone, who is there left to cheat, if the heart grows hard, life is the left in defeat. When reality is an embarrassment to condone, love's reaction never turns to stone. Sign on the dotted line, turn your heart and head for home, when the heart is nourished, the soul knows it's not alone, and the heart and the soul grow closer to the dawn. Take me to the place where the heart finds its fortune walking with you, talking with you, looking at an affinity with you. I know I'm on a course through torture looking at the world; cursing the truth, will it ever learn in this world there is a love to nurture and to savor the taste of love that is in your soul. The cost of freedom isn't worth a plug nickel anymore. Life is too important for a soul to be fickle, why give up now when wavering wouldn't cure; it's time to lay the sickle. Long-lost love stands in the circle. And the cure is so profound every soul is certain that love is found. Could this be the final calling? Love has the strength to serve a solution, deliver your hand to my conclusion. You will see that He healed our wounds, and they no longer can cause us harm anymore. As the cost of love is bought within the price of love's selfless goal. This is my love; listen to the sound, walk through the barrier, receive my reward, doubts clouding the truth, visions about to be restored. In this liaison with love, grace is the justice, and fortune for your heart in love's selfless goal, as we grow closer to dawn.

May the Lord bless all with love, faith, and enlightenment that hear these words in Jesus's name, amen.

PART FOUR

Summer 1989

July 1989: After Being Made Redundant

It's summertime in 1989; Patrick has flown to California to spend some time with his family. While there, he shared his lyrical prose with his niece, April, and her friend John. Both John and April enjoyed Patrick's lyrics, especially John Fluheart, who asked Patrick for a set of copies so he could share them with some musicians that he knew. Patrick agreed and got some copies for him.

A couple of months later, when Patrick was back home in the northeast of England, he had received a phone call from John, telling Patrick that the band, Guns n' Roses, wanted to purchase the rights to Patrick's lyrics.

Although during this visit and before Patrick had returned to England, he purchased a 1962 Mk 2 Jaguar and had it shipped to Felixstowe in England. Patrick then went to Felixstowe and drove the car home to the northeast of England. Patrick then acquired some quotes for the restoration of the vehicle. The cost of the restoration was far too expensive, but because the vehicle was a California car, there was no rust. And all three of the people who came to estimate the rebuild had offered to purchase the car, so Patrick sold the car for 150 percent profit. And the person that bought the car said that he would buy more vehicles like this one. Patrick then decided to become a self-employed importer.

Early 1990 Footballers: Before and After the World Cup Finals

As a result of this change of career, Patrick had become an importer of classic cars and vintage guitars, and this enabled him to travel back and forth to California over the next three years. And at this time, Patrick had become involved in a joint venture agreement with a young footballer called Paul Gascoine, otherwise known as Gazza, an extremely famous young man from the northeast of England who was considered as one of the best soccer players in the world.

Gazza had heard about Patrick's import company, JCP Imports, through his best friend, Jimmy "Five Bellies" Gardner, who was an apprentice mechanic where Patrick had brought some of the vehicles that he had imported from California to be repaired.

After taking Paul and his dad to look at a classic Jaguar E-Type Roadster and a Mark 2 at a dealer's premises in Beamish, the Aston Workshops, the owner had quoted the price of the two vehicles to Pat. When the owner had realized who the prospective customer was, he raised the prices by a considerable amount. Patrick made Gazza and his dad aware of this and said that if they wanted these vehicles, he would be able to purchase them in the United States and deliver them at a price even cheaper than what he had been originally quoted before for the two vehicles. And after having driven Patrick's 1952 Pontiac Chieftain from the Aston Workshops and around Gateshead, Paul picked up some of his various friends to take them for a ride in this old classic.

After a while, Paul drove the car to Patrick's house and waited on the driveway while Pat went to fetch his son, who was a massive fan of football and especially loved Gazza.

Gazza met Christopher and had a conversation with him, and at the end of the conversation, he said to Christopher that he was going to go into business with his dad, buying classic cars and importing them into Britain for resale. "Just like your dad is doing now."

Patrick was surprised by this and talked with Gazza later that day, and they agreed to go into business together. And shortly thereafter a contract for a joint venture agreement was reached and signed by both parties after a meeting in London with Paul's solicitor, Mel Stein, and agent Len Lazarus, a joint bank account was established with Barclays Bank in Newcastle Upon Tyne.

One evening, after the World Cup Finals in Italy, Gazza phoned Patrick and asked him if he wanted to join him for a drink at the pub. This was just after Gazza had returned from the World Cup finals in Italy. Patrick went to the pub and joined Gazza and Gazza's brother Carl and another group of soccer players and friends of Gazza. At one point during the evening, Paul ordered a wine cooler, diamond white cider snakebite, and gave it to his brother and told him it was juice: "Drink down in one, and it will pull you back together." Carl drank it in one and felt like he had been hit by Mike Tyson. Then Patrick watched Paul get another one at the bar and offer it to him; Patrick said, "Paul, I watched you pull that one on Carl, and then I saw you get that one from the bar. I'm not going to drink that after I saw what it did to Carl, go give it to Five Bellies," and they both laughed.

After a while, Gazza introduced Patrick to an eighteen- or nineteen-year-old football player, saying that this kid scored a hat-trick against Arsenal on his debut.

Pat said, "Wow, that's amazing."

Paul said, "This is Alan Shearer."

The two shook hands, and Alan and Patrick sat together for the rest of the night, drinking pints of beer and having a conversation about football and how Alan would like to attain a similar status that Gazza had attained.

After a while, Alan had brought up his most heavily weighted desire, which was to become a famous soccer player and to be able to play for England like his hero, Gazza. Alan was sticking like glue to Patrick after Paul had introduced him as his business partner and manager.

After a while, Patrick was getting fed up with Alan repeating his desire. Patrick then said to Alan, "Listen to me, I know that Gazza introduced me to you as his business partner, but I don't really work for Gazza, nor indeed do I even really work for myself either. I do have a partnership and a friendship with Paul. But I'm telling you now that I work for the Lord first and foremost, and the Lord has told me that you will become a very famous footballer, and you will play for England, you will even captain the English team in the future, buddy, so don't worry about this anymore, and you need not to mention it again, consider it a done thing. I'm telling you the truth; do you believe in Jesus?"

Alan replied, "Aye; yes, I do."

Patrick said, “Well, this is your destiny, brother. I’m glad that I’ve met you because you have a pretty cool future to look forward to, and you are a nice young man and very likeable, so put it there, buddy,” shaking hands, “let’s enjoy the rest of the night; what would you like to drink, Alan? I’ll get these.”

October 2009 Betrayal: A Little Deception and a Lightning Rebuttal

Patrick had brought all the paperwork from his court case on December 19, 2004, for his niece to type out on her laptop and to put the documents on a stick for later use, and he offered to pay her well for the job, basically so she could make some extra money. Malcom is now watching Patrick as he answers the phone; the call is from his niece. She had previously been speaking with her friends about going to the Creamfields Festival for the weekend with about fourteen of her friends. Stephanie could not afford to go to the festival, so she had a discussion with her pals and came up with the idea to con her uncle Pat into paying her for the task of typing the courtroom-documented testimonies of the harassment case that St. Ives Peterborough had brought against Patrick and had tried to have Patrick O'Malley charged with but failed in doing so.

Stephanie told her uncle that she had finished typing those documents and read the last couple of pages over the phone and explained that she just needed to get a memory stick and could she have the two hundred and fifty pounds that you said you would pay for the hundred or so pages of text? Patrick replied yes and said, "I'm so glad that you have finished that, as that stuff is submitted evidence as court testimony of a lot of the acts of faith that I foretold in Jesus's name. I'll bring the money over straightaway, sweetheart."

Patrick then later found out on the day before the festival was due to start that Stephanie's friends had advised her to lie to her uncle, and she hadn't done the job at all. Patrick is now looking up the Creamfields Festival on his wife's iPad. Patrick finds the geographical location on the iPad and says to the Lord, "This is the place," pointing onto the iPad. Patrick says, "Oh, Almighty God, send a mega storm to this place and cause the festival to be cancelled for this betrayal, and let loads of lightning crash onto the ground near Stephanie's friends and scare the hell out of them, and let them know that they gave Steph bad advice."

The storm came just before the festival started and completely flooded the Creamfields site, and the festival was cancelled and vacated. And as well as that happening, Stephanie had also contracted an extremely painful toothache that kept her in bed for the entire weekend, while her friends experienced the storm that Patrick had asked the Lord to send them there in response to their deceptions and had to leave the venue, as it was cancelled because of the storm.

Early 2005 York Mailing: A Job for Life? This Is Hanger Five from WWII

Patrick is now sitting at a boardroom table directly across from Mr. Newbould. Mr. Newbould is saying, "You have a job here for life if you want it, but I don't want to hear about any shenanigans. I've heard all about what happened at St. Ives, the letter, the lightning prophecy; well, I don't believe in God, I believe in money. So, keep your nose clean, and if you do, then you have a job for as long as you want. If I hear anything that merits dismissal, then I will be the one to fire you personally. You can start as soon as you are ready; I'll take you to the pressroom manager, and you can give your details to his secretary."

Malcom is now observing Patrick as he gets home from his first week working at York Mailing, saying to his wife, "Wow, June, I thought that I was going to work in York, but the place turns out to be Jamaica instead."

June replies, "What do you mean?"

Patrick said, "Well, one of the lads asked me where's the last place that we went for a holiday, and I told him, 'Amsterdam.' So, this guy says, 'Oh, so you must like the doob.' And I replied, 'Aye, mate, I don't mind having a smoke every now and then.' So, this lad says, 'Okay, let's go for a bifter at break time.' I said, 'Aye, okay, that's cool.' So, about an hour later, we go outside to have a cupper, probably around one in the morning."

June says, "So?"

Patrick says, "So we go out, and there's about another dozen that come out with us, and every one of them had rolled a joint and stood in a large circle and every one of them wanted me to take a toke off their spliffs."

June said, "Well, did you?"

Patrick says, "Well, yeah, I did, you know that I must become all things to all men."

June said, "You always say that to excuse yourself for going overboard, so then what happened?"

Patrick replied, "I got really, really stoned."

June said, "You idiot."

Patrick said it smelt like party night on a Jamaican beach and laughed his head off.

A bolt of lightning hits the factory a few months after Patrick started working at York Mailing. Mr. Newbould asks Patrick if he had anything to do with that incident. Patrick replied, "No, I don't think so, Mike, it's probably just a coincidence," while thinking, *Shit, I really need this job, I can't afford to get fired again, Lord Jesus.*

After a little while Patrick said, "Oh, Lord, did I ask you to send that bolt of lightning here recently?"

"Yes, you did. You know you asked; don't be fearful. You did say, 'Lord there's quite a few evil twats that work here, send a bolt of lightning, Lord,' so I did as you asked me. You are the one that holds the spear, just point it and ask, it shall be done, as you well know."

Lightning Never Strikes Twice in the Same Place, or Does It?

Patrick is outside of his house, having just arrived from the doctor's surgery, having just found out that he has high blood pressure due to stress that he's experienced at work being affected by the high level of evil being practiced there.

Patrick becomes very angry and says out loud, "I remember well that the wind is my friend, and the clouds are my friends, the rain is my friend, and the thunder and lightning are my friends. Oh, Lord, send a bolt of lightning to York Mailing like you did at St. Ives Peterborough, and cause the factory to lose the electrical power and bring the production to a standstill. And when they have got everything back online, well, you know how they say, lightning never strikes twice in the same place, so when everything is up and running, oh Lord, send a second bolt of lightning to the factory and knock everything out again in Jesus's name, amen."

Patrick is now crossing over with his shift opposite, pressman Robert Keane. Robert is visibly shaken and says, "Did you give it the shoes, did you shake off the dust from your shoes?" Patrick says no. Robert says, "Do you know what happened?"

Patrick says, "Yes, a bolt of lightning hit the factory, causing the presses to go down."

Robert says, "Do you know what happened after that?"

Patrick says, "Yes, a second bolt of lightning hit the factory and caused the power to fail again. Yes, Robert, I knew that, as I had asked the Lord to do that exact same thing earlier today, mate. Although you have nothing to fear, buddy; it's not about you. It's about this place, so calm yourself, mate, and don't be afraid. You know me, Robert, when I get confronted by enough evil to really get me wound up, then bang, here comes the lightning manifestation to remind demons that I have more power in God's Holy Spirit through Jesus's name than they can withstand."

2008: Chris Ingram Spits Out His Dummy

Patrick is now being observed sitting in a chair at the control counsel of a large printing machine, resting after five hours without a break, being five men short between two presses, where Patrick did his utmost to cover the work that needed to be done to keep the presses running. The CEO walked in the factory from the rear entrance and from behind Patrick, and as he passed by, he punched the back of the chair that Patrick was sitting on, causing the chair to move forwards. Patrick jumped up immediately saying, "What was that?" and then saw Chris, the CEO, standing a short distance away, motioning with his hand and index finger to get up.

Patrick followed Mr. Ingram and caught up with him and asked him if he had kicked the chair or had punched it?

Mr. Ingram replied, "I punched the back of the chair."

Patrick then said, "Did you hurt your hand?" He said no. Patrick then said, "Well, you did hurt my back, and I am going to make a complaint to the health and safety representative about that." The man then went off with a lot of anger and drove his sports car away at breakneck speed.

Patrick is now being harassed by the management because of the complaint that he made against the CEO. Patrick is now being observed going outside to his car at the end of his night shift. Patrick stopped momentarily outside and then asked the Lord out loud, saying, "Lord, you have seen how they persecute me because of my witness in serving your will; therefore, bring a bolt of lightning here today, and let these people know that you are with me and not them, in Jesus's name I pray, oh Lord."

2008 Ian: A Real Nice Man and a Friend

Ian Pagan, whom Patrick had known since Ian had started as an apprentice at Hunterprint when he was a sixteen-year-old, was also the son of Jimmy Pagan, who also worked with Patrick. Ian, now the pressroom manager, is talking to Patrick on the phone, asking him if he could work overtime, as a bolt of lightning hit the factory and caused a lot of downtime.

Patrick replied, "I know, Ian; I told you yesterday that you would see what you had heard about me for yourself, my friend. I am sure you remember when I asked you if you have knowledge about the full armor of God the other day, and you replied, 'Of course, I was a Jehovah's Witness when I was younger,' and it was then that I told you that the Lord had a spear from which lightning would proceed, reserved for one who would wield it in the latter days; well, dude, now you know what I am and who I am. So, I asked the Lord Jesus what was the reason why I had asked for the lightning to strike five times here, and then my Lord delivered them. It seems like a bit much for one factory. So, Ian, do you want to know what he said?"

Ian replied, "Yes."

Patrick then said that the Lord said that He was keeping his perception and aim sharp and true to strike into the heart of evil. "So, Ian, you know this place has a good bit of evil going on, this old aircraft hangar. A lot of shit has happened here, like the ghosts that loads of the lads have seen and the two rolls of paper, over a metric ton in weight each, that just started rolling on the flat floor right in front of three blokes as they were looking right at them, saying, 'What the fuck,' one of those three blokes being me. Then there was that three-quarter-filled trash bin at the sheeter end of press two that just lifted itself into the air about three feet and turned onto its side, hitting the ground with force, causing the rubbish inside of it to spread for a distance of about thirty-five feet right in front of Brian and myself, which totally freaked Brian out and scared the shit out of him. You were on shift that night, weren't you?"

Ian replied, "Yes, I was."

"Then Mark hired that dude, Darren; do you know what he said to me, Ian, he said that he's possessed by the devil. I asked him if he wanted to be exorcised; he said 'yes,' then he said 'no,' and kept repeating that over and over again and eventually settled on no, after two shifts in a row. And then Satan did his work through Darren. With Darren going to the management with lies trying to say that I was threatening them with divine vengeance through the invocation of the scriptures, according to my faith, and that is what really ruffled their fears."

Mike Newbould has just sold all his controlling shares in the company to Mr. Ingram. Patrick is now being observed in the board-room, being questioned by the management, namely Mike Newbould's two sons, about his faith. And about what happened at St. Ives in detail and about the lightning strikes that hit the factory. Tony asked Patrick if he asked the Lord to send a bolt of lightning to hit the factory.

Patrick replied, "Yes, and if you look at the closed-circuit camera in the front car park, you will see me standing outside, speaking out loud, looking upwards, and motioning with my hands, and bringing my right arm down, pointing at the ground. If you have an audio capability with your camera, then you yourself can hear me ask the Lord to bring a lightning strike to York Mailing today, in Jesus's name. And furthermore, I also told Ian Pagan that I was going to ask the Almighty to do this."

Tony turned towards Ian, seated at Patrick's left, and asked him if this was true? Ian replied yes.

Then Tony's brother said, "You shouldn't be allowed to work in industry here or in America or anywhere else for that matter because you are dangerous to business."

Patrick replied, "You shall see a massive worldwide recession starting from the moment that I give it the shoes, outside of here today." York Mailing made an audio recording of the entire meeting, which was also submitted to ACAS for the tribunal to take place in Leeds, Yorkshire thereafter.

Going Home for Christmas 1991: New Year's Eve and the Politician

Patrick is at Adolfo's apartment in Hollywood, and Freddie Onassis and a girlfriend come over for a visit for the second time in a week. Freddie and Patrick got on really well the first time they met, and Freddie asks Patrick what he's doing for Christmas. Patrick says that Jose Garcia and his wife asked him if he would spend the holidays at their house and look after their sixty birds while they're in San Salvador doing a documentary, and they are also using two of his poems, "The Children's Need" and "Stop the Genocide". "I declined the offer, although I'm very pleased that they want to use my lyrics to influence the people of San Salvador and Nicaragua to make peace."

So, Freddie then said that the family had a new yacht being built that would be ready for Christmas, "And I would be very happy and delighted if you could be our guest for Christmas and the New Year's celebration."

Patrick replied, "Wow, man, that is very cool and very generous of you to offer, but I'll have to decline, as I am going to England for the holidays, as I haven't seen my wife and son for eight months, and I couldn't disappoint the family, although I would have loved to spend the holidays with you and your family, Freddie. I don't think anything other than seeing my son could have persuaded me otherwise."

Patrick has arrived back to his home in the northeast of England, spending the Christmas and New Year's holiday with his family and friends. On New Year's Eve, Patrick and June went to the town of Sedgefield to celebrate the New Year with their friends, Brian and Alison Lister. Brian and Alison had previously lived in Whickham until Brian had got a promotion and took the position of general manager of Metro Radio's new station TFM on Teesside. There was a knock on the front door at approximately between eight and half-eight, that Patrick had opened at Alison's request. Patrick opened the door to three people, those being a Mr. Tony Blair, the local MP in England's parliament, and his wife, Cherie, accompanied by the local Catholic Bishop. Patrick led them through to the lounge, where quite a varied bunch of people were gathered. After a little while, Patrick noticed that nobody was conversing with the three people he had just greeted at the front door, so he started a conversation with the three of them and discussed Christian morals and the interaction that could be brought into government with a committed Christian leadership in Parliament. Whereupon Patrick asked Tony Blair if he wanted to become the Prime Minister, to which he replied, "No."

Patrick said, "I think you do want to become the Prime Minister, and I think that the Lord also wants you to become Prime Minister, and this could be very good for Britain; this will depend on you and your focus, try to do a good job of it, mate. And try not to be seduced by power and the darkness that surrounds it. There are a lot of evil people out there possessed by the love of money who will try to influence others in the place of authority, such as those that hold a position as a head of state, so try to be very astute and honest and focused on godliness, when you get there."

January 8, 1992, Palmdale and Valencia: Off with the Shoes

Patrick is at his sister's house, having just arrived from England, where he spent the Christmas holiday and New Year. Linda says, "There is a telegram here for you."

Patrick says, "Read it."

Linda says, "It's from your employer; it says that they have fired you."

Patrick says, "Really, let's have a look. Oh well, I'm going to go to the factory and see what this is all about."

Patrick is now at the office of the owner of London Press, saying to Mr. Gianmarco, "What's the problem; why do you want to fire me? Are you unhappy with the modifications that I had done with the folder that enabled us to speed up the production?"

Mr. Gianmarco said, "No, I'm very happy with that."

Patrick said, "Are you unhappy about the production and quality?"

He replied, "No, I'm very happy about that."

Patrick said, "Well, what's the problem then?"

"Well, the press hasn't run the whole time that you have been gone. Eric said that it must be something that you did before you left."

Patrick said, "The press was running in good order when I finished my last shift before going back to England to spend Christmas and the New Year with my wife and son. Eric is full of bull pucky and inexperienced, having only a year and a half of printing experience, whereupon I have had twenty years' experience, which also includes being a qualified installation, demonstration, and service print engineer and also an English union journeyman web press printer. Just give me my job back, and I'll get the press running properly."

Mr. Gianmarco said, "Eric also said that he found an empty beer can in the trash."

Patrick said, "That's a load of bull puck as well; Eric's trying to cover his own back because he's inexperienced to a degree, just give me the job back, and I'll get the press running again."

Mr. Gianmarco said, "No."

Patrick said, "Well then, in my opinion you are less than half a man."

Gianmarco jumped up and said, "Get the fuck out of my office."

Patrick said, "Don't worry, I'm going." Patrick walked out of the office towards the reception area as Mr. Gianmarco followed closely. Patrick stopped suddenly and said, "Oh yeah, there's one more thing that I need to do." Patrick then took off his shoes and jumped up as high as he could with a shoe in each hand and threw them down on the floor as hard as he could and said, "'Vengeance is mine,' says the Lord, 'I will repay,' and you will understand that. And I might even call the cops and tell them about the underage model that you had reprinted when you found out that she was underage, where you just had her face removed and then reprinted the rest of her naked body like some pervert."

At this point, Mr. Gianmarco started screaming towards the shop door for Michael, who at the time was married to an actor called Linda Gray, and for another lad, screaming like a girl, "Help!"

Patrick said, "Don't worry, I'm not going to hurt you; I do not use violence to settle a score. I use my faith in God to settle my scores, dude." Patrick then took a few steps towards the receptionist and asked her if she was due any vacation time?

She said, "Yes, two weeks, why Pat?"

"The Lord is going to bring a flood here out of nowhere, and you won't be able to get to work anyway. This is going to happen in four weeks, so book your vacation then. It's been a pleasure knowing you, Kathryn," saying goodbye, and then he left the premises.

Patrick is now back at his sister's apartment in Palmdale. He told his sister what happened at work and said that he was going to go back to the factory at the shift changeover and have a word with Eric. "I am so angry that I feel like breaking my vow of nonviolence and kicking Eric's ass, honestly that guy is a real asshole, he says that he's a spiritualist and a Scientologist and a surfer. I'm just feeling like knocking him out."

Linda said, "Oh Pat, don't break your vow of nonviolence, you made that vow to the Lord."

Patrick said, "Aye, you're right, Linda Lou, but I'm still going there to have a word with Eric."

Patrick's mother was sitting at the table with a cup of coffee and said, "You better not break your vow and fight with him."

Patrick said "Okay, Mom, don't worry; I won't. I shouldn't have said that, I'm just so angry about this situation and that asshole!"

Patrick is now at the factory car park waiting for the shift change. All the assistants came out and waited near their cars when they saw Patrick was standing in the car park near Eric's small pickup truck, and all of the lads that had arrived for work waited outside as well, near their cars. Patrick spoke to a few of them and asked them where Michael was, "my number two." Jose said he quit. Patrick said, surprised, "Why did he quit?"

Jose said, "He was told that they were going to fire you by Michael Gianmarco, and he said, 'If you are going to fire Patrick, then I quit right now,' and walked out the door and said to us that he wouldn't be working for them because they intended to fire you. We all know how he feels; we feel the same. All the guys love you, brother, but we can't afford to quit our jobs like Mike.

Oh man, I don't believe that Mike would quit his job, Patrick thought. *Well, Lord, I did ponder the possibility that Mike was an angel, as he is an extremely nice person; Jesus, bless him with further grace from your hand, oh Lord.*

At that moment, Eric came out the door, and the conversation stopped. Patrick followed Eric to his vehicle and had a conversation with him regarding his actions and accusations concerning Patrick. Eric had no justification except for the alleged empty can of beer and couldn't even look Patrick in the eye.

Patrick then said to Eric, "Well, you say that you are a spiritualist, a Scientologist, and a surfer. Well, I am a Christian with faith in Jesus's name, and I am telling you that you are going to need your surfboard to get out of here, so you had better start bringing it with you every day when you come to work."

Eric then got into his LUV pickup truck and drove off. Patrick then went back to the lads and said his goodbyes. The guys were all saying that they were going to miss him, and how much of a jerk that Eric was, and how they disliked him so much. Patrick told them about the conversation that he had with Eric and said to all of them that they should remind Eric that he should bring his surfboard to work. "Say to him, did you bring your surfboard with you today; you know that Patrick said that you're going to need it to get out of here. Do this because it will really wind him up and piss him off!"

Patrick then got into his mother's car to go back to his sister's apartment, and as he approached the driveway, Michael Gianmarco drove into the car park and blocked the driveway so that Patrick couldn't leave. Patrick got out of the car and walked over to the big, black Range Rover.

Michael stayed seated and opened the driver's window and started shouting, "You don't threaten the company, you don't call the cops, and my father said you threw your shoes down and said 'vengeance is mine, says the Lord,' what's all that about? My dad and I go to church every Sunday."

Patrick retorted, "So you think that gives you and your dad faith; well, as far as you're concerned, I'm just some nutter from England; now let me tell you what real faith is all about. I have asked the Lord to do these five things in Jesus's name, and the first thing that will happen is that a storm shall come out of nowhere, and flooding will happen on a large scale; then there will be riots sparked by police brutality, and then fires, and then an earthquake will come, followed by a second storm with flooding bigger and larger than the first storm. And all these things will happen in just over two years. And when these things have happened, both you and your dad will wish that you had never treated me the way that you have. Because you believed Eric's tainted story that is far from the truth, therefore making a misjudgment about me. Like I said to your dad, 'Vengeance is mine,' says the Lord. When all these things happen, you will truly understand that the Lord is with me!"

Late Summer 1984: The Rider and Seven Years Later

One day Biffo, the reel stand operator, had asked Patrick if he thought that he would still be working here at Hunterprint in the next ten years. Patrick replied, "Nobody will be working here in ten years' time, and, my friend, the only thing that I am sure of is that in roughly seven years I will be in California to do the Will of God."

Patrick was reading his Bible in a villa in Albufeiro on his own after his wife and son had gone for a swim in the Montechoro's hotel swimming pool. And then Malcom watched Patrick leave his body and observed him as he was translated to a mountainous area, where he had observed a man on a white horse who was wearing shining armor like the knights of medieval times and was armed with a sword and a spear that was harnessed on the right side of the horse, who had suddenly appeared on the dirt path that was in front of Pat. The mounted man approached what looked like a tunnel or a cave entrance. As he entered, demonic carved images could be seen; the rider drew his sword immediately and struck through the ceiling of stone, and the ceiling collapsed outwardly. And then he rode a bit farther along the path, until he had approached the end of the path and onto the precipice, very high and above the tree line, when suddenly an image of what looked like a female spiritual being, comprised of a blue shimmering translucent outline, appeared. The rider drew his sword and started to swing it towards her. She put her hands forward, gesturing as if to say *no*, whereupon the rider stopped. The entity pointed straight ahead; the rider could see a large, somewhat translucent dome protruding over the forest, whereupon he drew his spear and pointed it towards the dome. And immediately a bolt of lightning proceeded from the spear, and it hit the dome and destroyed it. Then Patrick's spirit returned to his body. And he said, "Wow, who was that guy, and what was all that about? I'm sure the Lord will reveal the meaning of this vision to me in His time."

Patrick then made his way to the hotel's swimming pool and joined his wife. He watched his ten-year-old son swim with some other boys about the same age. The boys decided to dive off the ten-foot-high mounted springboard, and after taking a good couple of dives each, one of the boys, Scot Semple, had decided to try to dive backside first, and he jumped off the board backwards and hit his chin on the edge of the springboard, on the way down into the water. He was knocked unconscious before he had even hit the water. Patrick saw this and immediately ran towards the pool, dove in towards Scot, and tried to pull him off the bottom of the pool, yet he found it very hard to lift the boy. Fortunately, another man had also seen what happened and was soon next to Patrick, and the two of them managed to get the boy out of the pool and laid him down on the poolside. Patrick's wife, June, who had extensive health and safety training, had also seen what had happened and took over the situation; she made sure to get the lad revived and also stopped the extensive bleeding from his chin, and Scot survived the accident and was returned to his parents, who were totally unaware of what had taken place but were extremely thankful and grateful that these people, strangers to them, had saved their son's life. June was a very special lady who had had a great career as the head of marketing and publicity for Gateshead Libraries and Arts and was instrumental and responsible for the budget as well that brought the Angel of the North, the Millennium Bridge, the Baltic Mill art gallery, and the Sage Gateshead music venue to the area during the regeneration of the Gateshead and its quayside on the Tyne River.

January 11, 1992: Roughly Seven Years Later

Patrick could then be seen on a dirt path with Franky and his brother Randy near some rock formations back in the Santa Monica mountains in California as they approached what looked like a large, hollowed-out boulder with a hole bored through the top. On the dirt floor are the ashes of a long-time burnt-out campfire; on the walls are demonic carved images. Patrick and his two companions, Franky and Randy, are looking for places to rock climb and to do some bouldering. Patrick tells them to go on, and he'll catch up with them in a bit. Patrick is now no longer interested in climbing, as he has become extremely annoyed by the carved images, to the point where he takes the shoes off his feet three times outside of the cave and shakes the dust off of them, each time saying, "'Vengeance is mine,' says the Lord, 'I will repay.' The first time that he shook off the dust of his feet, he said, "Oh Lord, send a mighty storm out of nowhere." The second time he asked the Lord to bring an earthquake, and the third time he asked the Lord to send a second storm larger than the first. "And let these be a sign from you, oh Lord in heaven!"

He then returned inside and peed into the long-time burnt ashes while circling the campfire and asking the Lord to make every drop of urine to be represented by a humongous thunderstorm cloud and also to create a storm that would come out of nowhere. Patrick then asked the Lord to send a second stream of urine to represent the second storm, which will be larger than the first. A second stream of urine appeared just as Pat finished his prayer with precise timing, giving him a bit of a shock at the immediate manifestation to his supplication. Patrick jumped and then looked up and could see Frank laughing his head off while peeing through the borehole on the top of the boulder.

After these events had happened and when he was back in England, he watched a television interview with Bette Midler, after these five events had been declared as five separate national disasters that had happened in the state of California. Jay Leno, the interviewer, had said to her, what about those disasters, they were like something out of the Bible, whereupon Bette Midler retorted that they weren't like something out of the Bible, they were something out of the Bible!

February 6, 1992: Leaving America and Last-Minute Lyrics

Patrick is at Adolfo's house with the rest of the band, going over some lyrical ideas, when Adolfo gets a call from Danny Huston asking if he'd like to come over. Adolfo explained the situation, and Danny told him to bring the lads with him. Patrick is now in Danny's house again and meets his wife and her brother about an hour after they arrived. Her brother had explained that he had just finished his first part in a movie and wanted to drink a bottle of vodka to celebrate. There were about eight or nine people there at the time, and nobody wanted to drink the bottle with him until he asked Patrick, who thought, *I don't really like drinking too much,* but he was also thinking, *Try to be all things to all men in order to win some,* and he agreed that he would help him celebrate, and the two of them polished off the bottle in the kitchen, although Patrick had not drank nearly as much as Michael. Then some more people arrived, three or four female friends of Danny's wife, Virginia Madsen, an extremely nice and very attractive woman, even more than attractive, enough to challenge Helen of Troy in desirability. Patrick thought, as he watched her dance near the HiFi while playing the Three Tenors on a vinyl LP, and said to himself, "Now I know how David felt when he saw Bathsheba for the first time, what a nice-looking woman, although I won't be following that same path that David did."

At one point, Patrick asked Danny if they had good drainage at the property? Danny replied, "Yes, why do you ask, that's a bit of a strange question?"

Patrick said, Well, there's going to be a very large storm coming very soon, Danny."

Danny replied, "As a matter of fact, we do have very good drainage here, Patrick."

And then he sat at the table with the ladies and talked with them for the rest of the night until he went home at about half-three in the morning. One of these ladies, who was quite forward, said that she really fancied him and asked him if he would stay at her house in London for six months until she returned to London, as she had just arrived in California and would be in Hollywood working in the film industry for the next six months. Also saying that her friend, a blonde lady would be staying there as well, but don't worry, she will love you, too, and will be very happy if you do decide to stay there.

February 7, 1992: Airport Frolics

Frank Horne and Brian Coole pick Patrick up at the condo to drive him to the airport twenty-five miles away. It's 10:30 a.m., the flight is due to take off at 6:30 p.m., so they go to visit Raul at his apartment in Studio City. The three of them stayed with Raul for a couple of hours before Patrick was then seen talking to Raul Carnados outside of his apartment while Brian and Franky went ahead towards the car. The two of them were discussing some lyrical ideas for the band, Raul being one of the band members. After discussing "Talk of the Prophets" and "The Whip Grows Weary," Raul is saying outside of his front door how lucky Patrick was to be going back to England and getting away from the drought in Los Angeles, saying, "Man, there has been a drought in California, and it hasn't rained here for the last five years."

Patrick said, "Oh Raul, you know how we both believe in Jesus?"

Raul said, "Yes, you know that I believe, mate."

Patrick said, "Well, the Lord has told me that there will be a massive rainstorm coming really soon."

Raul retorted, "Don't say that, Patrick; it's blasphemy."

Raul continues, "Patrick, you are not a prophet.

Patrick says, "No I am just a cowboy compared to them, like a gringo gaucho out on the pampas just trying to keep the herd together."

Raul said, "No you're not a cowboy or a gringo gaucho either, mate."

"No, I'm not, my friend, but, as a matter of fact I'm so certain that I am able to say that I promise you in Jesus's name that these things will happen."

Raul said, "Dude, be careful, talk like that could be blasphemy. Anyway, how can this happen when there are no clouds here or anywhere near; the clouds are in England, Scotland, Scandinavia, and places like that?"

Patrick replied, "It doesn't matter where the clouds are; I can promise you in Jesus' name that this will happen."

Raul asked, "How is this going to happen?"

By this time the two of them were near the swimming pool, close to the apartment gates. Patrick said, "The Lord is going to reach out with His right arm like this,"—while moving his right arm in a circular motion—"and He is going to gather the clouds in His hand and then throw them from where they are across the planet to here, my friend, and people will say, 'Wow, where did this storm come from, it's like it just appeared out of nowhere,' and you, my friend, shall have the wind and the rain in abundance for at least five days and probably a bit more, and it will bring flooding with it like you haven't seen before." Patrick said furthermore, "I promise you again for the third time in Jesus' name, believe me, Raul, this will happen, and it will start after I have left American airspace."

Patrick then said goodbye to his friend Raul, and Raul said, "Once you get back home, could you please phone me, transfer charge, I'll pay for the call, I insist."

Patrick said, "Okay, buddy." Patrick did call Raul about a week after he arrived home, and Raul answered the phone saying, "No more rain, no more rain, no more rain, no more rain, no more rain," as the crowd at Woodstock had shouted years earlier.

Then he returned to the car where Brian and Frank were waiting. As he got into the vehicle, Frank said, "What were you saying to Raul outside when you moved your arm around in a circular motion and appeared to throw something?"

So, he related what he had told Raul. They then drove to Adolfo's apartment for a while to converse with him as well, and Patrick told Adolfo about what he had said to Michael Gianmarco about the five national disasters that would follow his departure, and then they continued to the airport.

The three of them are now at LAX airport waiting for his flight. Frank and Brian are with Pat, asking him if he would stay in LA for a few more days, and tried to persuade him to do so.

Patrick replies, "Have you guys already forgotten what I told you in the car, when we left Raul's house, about the storm that's coming? I can't wait a few days, as the airport will be closed in a few days due to this storm that will cause flooding everywhere, including the runways, in a few days. I have got to go back to England, so don't worry, I'll see you again, I love you guys."

Just then an announcement came over the Tannoy saying, "Could the last passenger, Mr. Patrick O'Malley, meet the stewardess at passport control?"

Whereupon Patrick hurriedly headed to passport control near the gate and met the stewardess. And the two headed towards the airplane, running towards the stairway out onto the tarmac, and boarded the aircraft.

Patrick was shown the way to his seat and sat down, and then he fell asleep almost immediately. And in his sleep, just before waking up, he saw himself in the sky without the aircraft appearing to fly eastward, while still seated on fresh air, and saw what appeared to be a very large, luminous, white right arm and hand moving in a circular motion, counter-clockwise, gathering clouds in His fist and then throwing them westward. At this point, Patrick awoke and raised his fist, saying, “Hallelujah, thank you, Lord,” knowing that it was done, and immediately upon that, the captain of the aircraft announced that we were now leaving American airspace, as he had related to Raul earlier that day.

The storm came to Los Angeles, and all these things happened, followed by the riots, the fires, and an earthquake, and that followed by a second storm larger than the first, as Patrick had prophesied to Michael Gianmarco and other various people that he had confided in.

1986, Malcom's Last Vision: Leviathan and Talking to Abendigo on March 13, 2023

In the town of Capernaum, near the Sea of Galilee, Patrick is talking to Abendigo, a ten-year-old boy who has accompanied his mother on a pilgrimage to the Holy Land from Australia. He is telling the boy about an out-of-body vision that he had thirty-seven years earlier in his life. How he then could be observed while sitting cross-legged on the floor in a villa near the beach in the Faro region of Portugal. It is late morning. Then suddenly, while Patrick is meditating on the Bible verses that he was reading, in the blink of an eye, he was no longer in the room; in an instant, he is on the top of a hill with a grassy surface, overlooking a bay.

Patrick is looking out at the sea, and he notices two oil tankers sailing about three quarters of a mile off the shore. Then suddenly, he sees an extremely large sea creature rise out of the sea, and although still partially submerged, it was very close to the two oil tankers. The sheer size of the creature that rose along the side of the tankers dwarfs them to the point that its appearance makes them look like a couple of toys! And then they rolled over and sunk under the huge wake that the leviathan created as it rose from the depths of the sea.

Patrick was still watching the beast as a small boat approached the creature. A man armed with what looked like a harpoon or spear got out of the boat, proceeded to climb onto the back of the creature, and started to stab it with the weapon. The leviathan flicked his tail and dispersed of the man who was attempting to stab him. Patrick thought that man should have been a lot more patient and used stealth to accomplish the task. He then immediately observed a second man board the beast; this time, the man was armed with a short sword. This man went a bit farther along the back of the leviathan and then started to stab the creature as well; suddenly, the man was also dispersed of by the tail. A third man also came and mounted the creature as well; he was armed with a large knife and a sword, and he also climbed along the back of the beast until he had reached where he thought the heart of the beast might be and then proceeded to stab the creature. The leviathan flicked the man off of his back with his tail yet again.

Patrick then said to himself that these guys are being a bit careless, they're going to have to be much stealthier and patient. Patrick then found himself on the back of the leviathan, armed with a sword. Patrick then made his way along the back of the leviathan with stealth, not taking random stabs at the creature. Patrick carried along until he reached the beast's left upper limb, where he thought the heart might be. He then climbed downwards to the limb and held onto the limb, using it to shield himself from the tail, as he repeatedly stabbed the creature. The leviathan flicked his tail and tried to dislodge Patrick. Patrick watched as the tail repeatedly tried to dislodge him, and he laughed while continuing to stab the beast. Patrick held on and continued to stab the leviathan until the tail had finally managed to reach him and dislodged him as well.

He then found himself back on the hill overlooking the sea, where he had first been translated to. Within a moment, a man dressed in leather approached Patrick and said, "We are going to go back onto the beast; now you follow me, and don't say anything; when I move, you move, follow every step I take." The man also said, "When we reach the back of the head, I'm going to jump twice; you jump when I jump, and stay very close to me; watch what I do, and move when I move." This man was armed with a large sword.

The two men were suddenly on the back of the leviathan like the others that went before Patrick. Then Patrick followed the Lord with his great sword without saying anything, as the Lord just motioned with his hand until they had reached the back of the leviathan's head. The man had motioned to Patrick to get ready, and Patrick could hear him in his mind saying, *When I jump, you jump and say nothing, just move when I move.*

There was a bit of cheekbone structure underneath the left eye of the beast, easily large enough for the two men to stand on; the eye was at least a dozen feet in diameter, possibly even larger. The two men jumped together as one, and the man dressed in leather immediately plunged His sword into the eye of the beast. Then he swiftly jumped onto the forehead of the leviathan again, immediately plunging the sword into a section of the forehead just above the level of the eyes, which were situated on the side of its head. The blood of the beast poured out in volume, causing the sea around it to boil with intensity.

This happened, and then Patrick and the man in leather were now watching from the grassy hill, where Patrick had first observed the creature. After seeing the beast die and sink back into the sea, Patrick returned to his body, and when he came back to his own reality, he said, "Wow, I've just seen the Lord himself kill the dragon that is in the sea, that old serpent called leviathan and the devil, hallelujah. I feel so humbled and blessed by the Lord to have become a part of His plan in some capacity."

And then he asked Abendigo if he liked that story; Abendigo said, "Yes, I love that story better than all the other stories that you have told me; that's definitely my favorite, Pat."

1991: Malcom's Vision Comes to an End

At this point, Malcom stood backwards a little bit and said, "You know what, you are right. I now agree with you because of this moment in time that I have spent with you. And I now feel that I have been enlightened, and I wholeheartedly agree with you, my friend." He continued to say, "I have met a lot of powerful people in my time; I have met political leaders, and I have also met various other religious leaders and other politicians from other countries, although you, my friend, you are the most powerful person that I have ever met."

Patrick replied, "Oh no, I'm not powerful at all; I'm just a simple man with faith in God."

Malcom then said, "No, you're not just a simple man; you are the most powerful man that I have ever met."

Patrick said, "Well, you are entitled to your opinion, but I don't see myself as that, my friend, not at all. I see myself as a servant of the Lord and nothing else, for I must decrease and He must increase, as that is the meaning of being crucified with Christ."

The two men walked back towards Patrick's cousin's condo, whereupon they stopped, hugged each other, and shook hands vigorously. As Malcom turned around to head back towards the 7-Eleven store, Patrick took a step towards his cousin's condo thinking, *Oh, I'll give him some cigarettes to take with him.* And then, upon turning around within a few seconds, Patrick was surprised to see that Malcom was nowhere to be seen, although when they turned away from each other,

Malcom was at least fifty to sixty feet from the edge of the 7-Eleven store, alongside the windowless brick wall. After looking around and across Sepulveda Blvd., Patrick thought he must have gone into the 7-Eleven store.

Patrick walked back to the 7-Eleven store and asked the shop assistants if they had seen the man that he had been talking with and if he had come into the store? The shop assistant replied, "We saw you and that guy walking and talking outside, but we haven't seen him since the two of you walked past the shop going east."

Patrick then went into the pizza shop and asked the assistants the same question; they told him the same answer that the guys from the 7-Eleven store had relayed. Patrick then went into the donut shop and asked the two lads in there the same question. They also replied with virtually the same answer as the other shop assistants. Patrick then walked back to his cousin's condo, thinking, *Wow, that was a very strange encounter.*

Mid-February 1992:
Who Was Malcom, Anyway?

Patrick is now back in England at his very good friend Taff's house; he had been telling Taff, whose name is actually Dr. Alan Hughes, and Ann, his girlfriend, all the things that had happened while he was in California over the last nine months.

Taff said, "Wow, Pat, that story is really cool and surprised me even more than that time when I went rock climbing in Wales, when I said to you, 'Guess what I found on the rock face yesterday?' And straightaway, you said, 'Oh dude, I know what you found; I knew yesterday that you found a white crystal in a purple suede pouch while you were climbing.' I can tell you that that really blew my mind, but these things are totally incredible, buddy."

Just then Patrick notices a book upside down on the chair side table. And on the back of the book's dust cover is a picture of the man that he met that night three-and-a-half months earlier on Sepulveda Blvd., halfway between the condo and the 7-Eleven store heading east. He turned the book over and said, "Bloody hell, wow, that dude was Malcom Little. How bizarre, that dude was murdered and passed away around twenty-six years ago. The good Lord must have reanimated him just for this purpose. That must be why he disappeared so suddenly after we finished speaking to each other. Wow, Lord, now that was something that I never expected would happen; thank you, Jesus, for that rare experience, although a lot of people will think that I might be a bit crazy when I tell them this story and about the rest of my witness into the faith of Christ, although the Book of Revelation does say, that the testimony of Jesus Christ is the spirit of prophecy. Amen."